PRAISE FOR
Radical Giving

"God has entrusted the church in America with unprecedented wealth, but we've largely missed His invitation to discover the abundant life of Christlike generosity. Dr. DeWitt has a remarkable story of discovering God's heart for radical generosity and then living it out in his own life. Those who embrace and model the principles he sets forth will discover a deeper relationship with Christ and a more joyful posture toward their finances. I'm grateful for this important work!"

—**JOHN CORTINES**, *COO, Generous Giving*

"I love the personal approach of this book. As the journey unfolds, I was drawn to imagine myself as part of the story. Each of the lessons being shared holds significant meaning. It will inspire every reader to give thoughtfully, intentionally, and generously. Be prepared to be transformed into a cheerful giver!"

—**JOE PRINGLE**, *President, National Christian Foundation, Chicago*

"Andy LIVES IT OUT! I am grateful for Andy, who gives insight into how we can worship God through stewardship of what He has entrusted to us!"

—**MARY L. PUDAITE KEATING**, *Generosity Strategist, Worship Leader, and Speaker*

"When it comes to generosity, Andy is radical—and I am thankful for that. Andy is showing the rest of us the way it should be. With humor and transparency, he shares his successes and failures in a way that will help all of us excel in the grace of giving."

—**RICH VANDERSANDE**, *Founding Partner, Smart Stewardship Advisors*

"Andy's book is a relevant and important contribution to the growing library of great resources in the stewardship and generosity space. You will be challenged and encouraged as you read this book. Andy is a guide to those of us who want to steward our one and only life to the fullest."

—**JEFF ROGERS, CKA®, CEP®,** *Founder and Chairman of Stewardship Legacy Coaching, LLC. Jeff is also a ForbesBooks featured author of the book* Create a Thriving Family Legacy: How to Share Wealth and Wisdom with Your Children and Grandchildren.

"This is an important book that tackles the hard questions about God and money. It will challenge your relationship with finances and bring your faith in our generous God to a deeper level. With wit and entertaining stories, Andy teaches the Bible's profound truths on money and shows practical ways we can worship God in our giving. His authenticity about his journey is both relatable and inspiring."

—**NEIL IHDE,** *Founder and President, Life IQ*

"This book takes a very personal approach, helping me imagine myself as part of the story as it unfolds. It was truly inspiring and has helped my wife and me act on making generosity a more integral part of our lives."

—**BRIAN SCHATZ, COO,** *Medical Associates of Dubuque*

"Convicting and practical, this is a book every Christian should read. The contrast between Jesus-oriented stewardship and our normal human-oriented mindset of money and giving is enlightening. Andy gives practical guidance to wrap our lives around Jesus through generosity."

—**TIMOTHY WILLIAMS, CPA,** *Controller, Foodliner*

"If you are struggling to know how to wisely steward the money God has entrusted to you, *Radical Giving* will help you navigate through the fog of uncertainty. This book will be an important resource for those who seek to advance the kingdom of God."

—**SHANU N. KOTHARI, MD, FACS, FASMBS,**
Fellowship Director of MIS/Bariatric Surgery,
Gundersen Health System

"With uncommon transparency, Andy provides a gospel-centered and practical perspective on giving. Regardless of your wage level or status, this book is your map for a life of generosity."

—**JONATHAN ZLABEK, MD, FSVM, FACP,**
Medical Director of Disease Management, and
Board of Trustees member, Gundersen Health System

"This is a book I will read over and over again. The idea that challenged me most is that we should not worry about tax deductions but give out of love for our Savior. It cost Jesus everything! I think we can give without worrying about the tax implications."

—**DANIEL ALLISON,** *Vice President, Managing Director*
of Key Accounts at Prudential Retirement; Pastor at
CrossRoads Church, Peosta

Radical Giving

How Remarkable Generosity Can Set You Free

Andy DeWitt

Publisher Name and Contact:
WML Publishing
15368 Stacie Ct.
Dubuque, IA 52002

AndyDeWitt.org

Scripture quotations are taken from the Holy Bible, New Living Translation, copyright ©1996, 2004, 2007, 2013, 2015 by Tyndale House Foundation. Used by permission of Tyndale House Publishers, Inc., Carol Stream, Illinois 60188. All rights reserved.

Paperback ISBN: 978-1-7326494-6-0
Ebook ISBN: 978-1-7326494-5-3

Interior Graphics by: Ryan Winkelman
Cover Design by: Amy Cole, JPL Design Solutions

Printed in the United States of America

To my three great kids, Alex, Aiden, and Abby.
May the godly inspiration of this book and the imperfect yet
faithful example of your parents inspire each of you to pursue
God's vision for your financial resources.

"I could have no greater joy than to hear that
my children are following the truth."
–3 John 4

CONTENTS

WHY I WROTE THIS BOOK

I'm not a financial expert or a teaching pastor, so why would I write a book on biblical stewardship?

My wife, Anna, and I have been following Jesus Christ as our Lord and Savior for many years. Early in our marriage, I had an experience with God that set us on a course to abandon the American Dream and pursue what some people might call *radical generosity*. We've been giving for over fifteen years now and have loved it; for a long time, though, we didn't share our story or teach about giving. Because the Bible says we shouldn't let our right hand know what the left hand is doing when we give (Matthew 6:3), I felt we were not allowed to talk about money. So I didn't. The result was that we were doing what God wanted for us financially, but we were isolated and alone.

A few years ago, I was invited to a Generous Giving conference in Atlanta. This was a unique weekend where tremendous speakers shared stories and taught on biblical generosity, but nobody asked for money. On the flight to the meeting, I read David Platt's book *Radical*. Among other things, Platt calls us to reconsider our finances and demolishes the concept of the American Dream. It is a selfish dream and it is not biblical. When I was halfway through the book, I closed it and placed it on my lap. It was time to think. I considered what I knew about giving and the Bible and compared it to what I had just read.

1

It was clear to me that the life Platt described as *radical* was nothing more than the life described in the Bible as *normal*. In fact, it was the life Anna and I were living!

I got off the plane and attended the conference. I heard stories from people who are striving to be generous in every way, and they had found a way to talk about generosity and teach about biblical stewardship of money without being smug or pretentious. It was still as if the right hand did not know what the left hand was doing. With this group, for the first time in my adult life, I felt normal with regards to our finances.

A few years have passed, and we've continued our personal journey of generosity. Over that time, I've come to realize that I don't need to live in isolation. I've shared my story a few times in small groups, and people seem to have been blessed by it. Along the way, I also picked up the hobby of writing books. I've written about mission organizations, and I scrawl out a fun novel for my kids for Christmas every year. One beautiful summer afternoon, my wife said, "You should write a book about giving!" I scoffed at the idea, having read dozens of books on the subject. I thought, *There is plenty of information out there on money. Why would I write about that?* The next morning, I woke up at 3:00 a.m. with several chapters already outlined in my head. I thought about my story, about being strategic in how we give, and about how our successes and many of our failures have imprinted lessons on my heart about the vast realm of generosity. I realized God had taken my wife and me on a journey of discovery in the area of giving, and maybe—just maybe—He wanted to me share what we'd learned along the way. This book is the record of that journey.

I pray you are challenged to hear how God would like you to handle the money He has entrusted to your care. So, with that in mind, I present to you my story.

CHAPTER 1

IT'S ALL ABOUT JESUS

The wicked borrow and never repay, but the godly are
generous givers.

Psalm 37:21

If this is the first book you've ever picked up about Christianity or Christian living, put it down and grab a different book. Let me suggest a few: *Not a Fan,* by Kyle Idleman; *Radical,* by David Platt; *Mere Christianity,* by C. S. Lewis; or any book by Francis Chan. These books teach a basic premise of having our lives completely dedicated to Jesus Christ. They also allow us to focus our hearts on Jesus and dispel the myth that, after you become a Christian, you can go on living your life just the same as before you knew Jesus. The simple fact is that a life committed to Jesus looks different than the average life.

THE AMERICAN DREAM

We could probably define the American Dream as having the freedom to pursue a better life than our parents and the hope that our kids will have a better life than ourselves. A generation ago, it meant having a house with a two-car garage, a stable job with a 401(k), and a white picket fence. Nowadays, you can replace the white picket fence with an underground electric dog fence, add in enough expendable income to pursue whatever hobbies make you happy, and hope that the forty-hour workweek will result in a comfortable retirement. Of course, there are as many variations of the American Dream as there are people who dream it, but one theme rings true: "I want more! I deserve more!"

American society is built on this dream. However, when we strip it down to its foundation, we see it is a prideful and selfish dream. Many problems stem from a society based on selfishness, and pride is at the heart of a myriad of sins. Living the way Jesus intends is the opposite of our self-centeredness. It is all about Him; it's not about us at all.

A heart that is wholly following Jesus is not guided by the same principles as a heart that's pursuing the American Dream. It is not running a race of economic success in order to get ahead. We cannot live a Christian life on our own terms. We need to strive to understand what kind of life God wants us to live and how He wants us to live it. This is done through reading the Bible and responding to the Holy Spirit.

When we are sold out to Jesus and the Holy Spirit takes residence in us, we change. This isn't a glossy, surface-level change that just makes us look good in front of other people; it is God working in us that brings about the deep character differences the people around us notice. Encouraging words flow more easily. A rough-and-tumble fighter can become a gentle teddy bear. We begin to reveal kindness, faithfulness, and self-control as hallmarks of our character. As the Holy Spirit produces the fruits of love, joy, peace, and patience in our lives, we are no longer the same (Galatians 5:22–23). Certainly, this is a process of redemption over time, and grace is needed because none of us live up to God's standard all the time. When we center our lives around Jesus, we start to emulate Him.

When our focus is on Jesus, the lens through which we view our lives changes. The God of the universe has so drastically changed our hearts that we pursue a life guided by a passion for Him rather than staying focused on ourselves. It is a visible and tangible difference that's seen in our dedication to prayer, our acts of service, and our relationship with money. Giving money is a big part of what Jesus wants for us.

We cannot earn our way into heaven—not by doing great things and certainly not by giving. We can't buy God's favor; Scripture is clear on that (Ephesians 2:8–9). Salvation is by faith alone, in Christ alone, and absolutely not by doing things that would earn our salvation. Rather, when our hearts are dedicated to Him, our habits change; we reflect Him more and more over time, and we end up living a life that makes Him smile.

The goal is pleasing our awesome God, not pursuing the American Dream. Now, where does that leave us when it comes to handling God's resources? We are stewards of our time, talents, and treasure. Every hour, any ability we have, every penny we have, everything He has blessed us with—all these belong to God. Our job is to *manage* it. We should constantly ask ourselves, *Am I a good steward of the assets God has given me? If not, what should I change?*

We are His representatives, and this is an important job. As we continually worship our amazing God, the next logical step is to create a plan for how to use our money based on Him and not based off our own aspirations or goals. The goal is to figure out what *He* wants to do with the money *He* has put in our care.

TYPES OF GENEROSITY

Generosity comes in many forms. Small towns across the country have volunteer fire departments full of skilled men and women who are committed to helping their communities. They know the small towns often can't afford a full-time fire department, so they generously give their time and work to save lives. Teachers who volunteer in after-school mentoring programs are changing the lives of students who have needs that only well-trained teachers can provide. Churches are full of volunteers who give their time freely: musicians, Sunday school teachers, and especially nursery workers use their talents for God's glory.

Those are great examples of people giving their time and talents, but what about our money? When we look at what the Bible says about finances, the most common starting place is the tithe. This just means giving one-tenth of your income to God, which is taught throughout the Bible.[1] We will unpack this more in Chapter 9; for now, it's enough to say it is clear that God calls us to give the first ten percent of our income.

For the Israelites, paying the tithe was simply something they always did; it was a normal part of their culture, just like paying sales tax is for us. In their agrarian society, they gave the first of their harvest. Today, we give our tithe first after receiving our paycheck, traditionally dropping cash or a check in the offering plate as it is passed during a Sunday morning church service. Modern banking bypasses this with monthly direct deposit and other digital means to routinely transfer money. These scheduled donations not only provide the finances necessary for the church to pay their staff, perform their ministry, and keep the lights on, but the process of regular giving does a tremendous work in the heart of the giver.

A senior pastor once noticed that his young associate pastor wasn't giving financially to the church at all. He asked him, "Why aren't you tithing to the church?"

The young pastor was expecting the question and responded, "When I took this job, I gave up a career making $80,000 a year to follow the call of God and work in ministry. I'm happy here, but I'm only making $45,000 a year. So I'm actually giving $35,000 every year."

The pastor responded, "You are generous with your time and talents, and I admire your sacrifice. However, that does not represent generosity with finances. You aren't tithing your first fruits. You're just saying, 'I used to have more fruit, so I shouldn't have to give.' God is still providing you with $45,000."

The young pastor sighed, "You mean I still have to tithe even though I'm already sacrificing?"

The senior pastor placed his hand on the young man's shoulder and said, "The heart that Jesus is looking for is the heart that looks at that salary with thankfulness, not regret, and gives from what God provides. Besides, in Numbers 18:26 the priests are instructed to tithe on their income."

We shouldn't confuse giving our time and talents with our stewardship of money. Maturity in the Christian faith is almost impossible to measure, but if we were to try, we could evaluate it as a chair with four legs: service, prayer, Bible study, and giving. All four are incredibly important, and there is much to say about serving God with our time and talents. Prayer is a topic needing unending discussion and practice, and it should *never* take a back seat to anything. Bible study is also essential; without spending time in His word, we can't know Him. However, in this book, our focus will be on the fourth leg of the chair: financial giving.

How Much?

When it comes to finding out how much we should give, there are no hard and fast rules. In his famous book *Mere Christianity*, C. S. Lewis explains it this way:

> I do not believe one can settle how much we ought to give. I am afraid the only safe rule is to give more than we can spare. In other words, if our expenditure on comforts, luxuries, amusements, etc., is up to the standard common among those with the same income as our own, we are probably giving away too little. There ought to be things we should like to do and cannot do because our charitable expenditure excludes them.[2]

Simply put, our giving should put some limits on our lifestyle spending. If you can buy whatever you want whenever you want without your giving getting in the way, Lewis would say you aren't giving enough.

God looks at money differently than people do. When I was a boy and got worked up about money, my wise and loving father would gently put his hand on my shoulder and say, "Money is just a medium of exchange." These wise words went far over my head for years. He was trying to get me to calm down and not expect money to solve my problems and to understand that money is just there for us to buy and sell stuff. It's not to be loved or hoarded. Many years later, I'm now the dad. I've been drilling my children: "There are three things we do with money: give, save, and spend." Before I let them manage any money at all, they needed to be able to repeat back to me the three things we do with money. This was my attempt to help them realize money is a useful tool for a lot of things, but it is not the most important aspect of life.

Luke 21:1–4 tells of Jesus and His disciples watching people put money into the collection box at the back of the Temple. Rich men pass by and add a large number of gold coins to the box, followed by a poor widow, who only gave two small copper coins. Before we get to what Jesus said, let's take a step back and look at some cultural aspects of this story. A widow in first-century Jewish society was among the poorest class of people. With no husband to provide for them, the widows generally couldn't work and were relegated to begging. If you search the Bible for stories about widows, you don't see rich, successful widows changing the world. You see women begging to stay alive. The Old Testament has several instructions to not exploit widows and commendations for providing them with justice.[3] These instructions were necessary because widows were generally poor and exploited. If a widow was fortunate enough to have money in her hands from selling something or earning it somehow, it was commendable and definitely needed. For her to give that money away would be unthinkable!

As Jesus watched the rich men and compared them to the poor woman, He said the most amazing thing about money:

> "I tell you the truth," Jesus said, "this poor widow has given more than all the rest of them. For they have given a tiny part of their surplus, but she, poor as she is, has given everything she has." (Luke 21:3–4)

Money reveals the heart. When a generous person receives an infusion of money, whether suddenly or over time, they don't change into a different person; they just become more of what they already were underneath. When a greedy person who has been into his or her hobbies comes into having even more money, what do you think will happen with his new finances? Their hobbies will get bigger and more overwhelming.

We usually don't have the opportunity to see past a person's façade to view their generosity or their greed. Consider a struggling African farmer who barely has enough to feed his family, yet he makes a habit of being generous with his neighbors and friends by giving them a small bundle of his crop of lentils. When his farming improves over time and he becomes more prosperous, what will happen to his pattern of using his harvest? He'll give more and larger bundles of lentils to more people. His generosity will expand, and he will do more and more to help his family and friends. This occasionally becomes apparent after someone receives a windfall of money, but God knows the heart before the change happens. For the Christian, every penny we spend reveals something about our relationship with God.

Jesus knew everything about the poor widow. He knew her limited assets and her monthly expenses. He also knew what was in her heart. Amazingly, Jesus declared to His disciples that she was more generous than any of them.

When we talk about generosity, we are not talking only to people who have wealth. It's easy to think that being generous only applies to people who have abundance, but everybody from a billionaire to the poor widow has the opportunity to give! Generosity is often noticed when people make substantial gifts, but everybody makes decisions every day on how to spend their limited money and has regular opportunities to give. In fact, many of the most generous hearts belong to those with meager resources.

The difference between a self-centered heart and a generous heart is how we choose to use the resources we already have. Where does it go? Do we enhance our wants and needs, or do we find ways to give toward the needs all around us? It's amazing how the definition of *wants* changes to *needs* when additional funds become available. When we get a raise, suddenly we can do more of the things we want to do—and we convince ourselves that we *need* to do/get/buy them. This is a normal thought process for everybody. It doesn't matter if you are on a fixed Social Security income, making minimum wage, or the average American with a household income of $50,000 a year. What would it look like if each of us thought about God's direction for our spending, giving, and saving first and our own desires second? I suspect we'd use our money much differently.

Again, money reveals the heart, and Jesus cuts through all our preconceived ideas about money in Luke 21:1–4. Yes, it is important to understand that it is a medium of exchange. Yes, it is essential to know that money is used to give, save, and spend. Most importantly, Jesus says our generous giving—whether given out of abundance or poverty—shows what is inside: hopefully a heart filled with the love of Jesus.

HOW DO WE LEARN
ABOUT GENEROSITY?

Where do we go to learn about giving? The biblical principle of the tithe says to give ten percent, and we can trust that. However, when the church teaches on giving in detail, they risk being called money grabbers and turning people off to church in general. As a result, many churches avoid the topic completely, except perhaps in classroom settings. Where, then, can we get educated on how to give generously? In the pages that follow, I hope to guide you through some processes that will help hone the skills of giving well. This book is not a how-to instruction manual for those who are struggling to get out of debt and attain financial freedom. Dave Ramsey has a fantastic program for that called *Financial Peace University* (daveramsey.com). In fact, the last point in Dave's Seven Baby Steps is to give generously. It's an effective plan, and the last step is the most fun of them all. In this book, we'll explore many of the aspects of that part of the financial journey: *giving generously*!

In this day and age, some families have incomes that far exceed their actual needs—the normal daily living expenses of a middle-class family. People have hobbies that cost an inordinate amount of money each month, and our ability to find ways to spend extra income is endless. It should be routine for people to step back from their personal lives and decide to redirect their income toward the kingdom of God in greater ways. It should not be uncommon for all Christ followers to be generous in many ways. And yet, sadly, it is.

Not just those with wealth, but all of us, in one way or another, have a tremendous opportunity to help others. Our influence, when coupled with experience and skillful giving, can allow the kingdom of God to extend beyond our neighborhoods, reaching out to other cities and countries. Our God is a generous, loving God. The premise of this book is that, once you have been transformed by the love of Jesus Christ, the way you handle money will reflect His love in your life. Together, we can dive specifically into what this can look like in our stewardship of money. How can we give better? How can we make a bigger impact? How can we make a plan to be generous?

Let's find out!

Looking inside:

1) What's your version of the American Dream?

    a.   What was your American Dream when you were a child?

    b.   What is your version of the American Dream today?

    c.   How does that compare to the life Jesus wants for us?

2) What does your financial picture look like?

    a.   Are you deeply in debt and struggling to make it month to month?

    b.   Are your finances under control and working for you?

    c.   Is it easier for you to give when you feel like your finances are under control?

3) What's the difference between giving your time, talents, and treasure?

    a.   Which is easier?

    b.   Which causes you to rethink your priorities?

Taking action:

1) If your finances are a mess, your first step should be to go through Dave Ramsey's *Financial Peace University* program. He will walk you through a process to take hold of your finances and make them work for you. You can learn more at daveramsey.com.

2) Should giving generously be the first or the final step in your financial plan?

    a.   What would happen if you started giving generously *before* your finances looked great on paper?

    b.   What could happen if you gave generously even in the face of poverty like the poor widow did?

CHAPTER 2

GIVING WITH AN OPEN HAND

Remember this—a farmer who plants only a few seeds will get a small crop. But the one who plants generously will get a generous crop.

2 Corinthians 9:6

I'm running errands from store to store downtown on a cloudless summer day. I have plenty of time to visit several of my favorite shops, which I usually do quickly and rarely enjoy. This time, however, it's actually a pleasure. I stop and notice an ice cream shop that I usually only visit when my kids are with me. I'm not in a hurry, so I decide to treat myself and walk through the door. I order a vanilla cone, pull a few dollar bills from my wallet, and give them to the teenager behind the counter. That's when I realize I've got a $20 bill I didn't expect to have. I smile from ear to ear. Perfect. In a rare moment of utter relaxation, I take a seat on an outdoor bench and enjoy the moment.

A man in torn jeans and an old shirt runs up to me. Frantically, he says, "I have to get to work, but my car has a flat tire. My normal commute is only fifteen minutes, and now I'm almost late. If I don't get to work on time, I'll lose my job."

I'm shocked. He continues talking about his wife and kids at home. At a loss for words, I only say, "I'm so sorry. How can I help you?"

He refocuses and says, "If I had $20, then I could get a taxi to work. Can you help me out? I just can't lose my job!"

His day is certainly not as perfect as mine, so I look into his eyes and smile. He looks genuine, and there is a real need right in front of me. I want to help, so I ask where he works and how he normally gets there. His story is totally reasonable, and he is obviously down on his luck. I pull my wallet out, give him the $20 bill, and feel magnanimous. I puff out my chest and smile, basking in the glow of my grand gesture.

Then, as he turns to go on his way, a spark of curiosity causes me to watch him hail his cab. Instead, as he heads around the corner, he looks like he has no intention of hailing a cab at all. At this point, I start to get a little suspicious, so I follow him at a distance. After another block, my ice cream melts down my fingers as I watch him head into a liquor store. He eventually comes out with a bottle in a bag.

In disgust, I throw my ice cream on the ground and blurt out, "I just gave that silver-tongued bum a bottle of alcohol!" Inserting my favorite self-deprecating slur, I continue, "He cheated me. He didn't need a taxi at all! That's the last time I help a stranger. I'm never gonna get burned like that again."

In a moment, my mood shifts from enjoying a peaceful, blissful day to anger and discouragement. Plus, I wasted a perfectly good ice cream cone! I had been burned. I gave unwisely. But did I really do anything wrong? Was his impropriety my fault? I don't have anything against buying a friend a drink, but that's not exactly what I want to do with the dollars I've designated for *giving*. If I were to do it all over again, what could I have done differently?

Put Jesus in the Picture

Now, let's imagine that same story with one significant change. Jesus Christ is there with me in person while I am running my errands. He rides shotgun in the car and then walks side by side with me down the street on that same beautiful day. Just for fun, let's have Him look the way He is drawn in children's picture books: long brown hair, beard, a white robe with a blue sash, and, if you wish, you can even picture Him with a lamb on His shoulders.

Jesus and I zip from store to store, and He helps me find the best deals. Everything I buy is on sale, and I get ideal parking spots because, you know, He's Jesus! Then, with ice cream in hand, we sit on the bench together talking away when the man in jeans and an old shirt tells his tale about the flat tire and how he needs to get to work. Jesus sits back and watches while I ask a few questions, pull out my wallet, and deliver my precious $20. I feel great and wonder if magnanimous is really a word.

I smile at Jesus, and He nods back. Jesus and I follow him down the street, and Jesus offers to hold my ice cream just before I watch the guy enter the liquor store. Jesus says, "It looks like he wasn't as innocent as it seemed."

As he exits with the bottle in a bag, I look at Jesus and say, "I just gave that silver-tongued bum a bottle of alcohol!" This time, I leave out the self-deprecating slur. "Why didn't you warn me he was a liar and a thief?"

Jesus puts His arm around me, and we turn and walk back down the street. "Well, he is a liar. But he's not a thief."

"He stole my money!" I cry.

"No, you *gave* it to him," Jesus smiles. "But you're partly right; you were burned. You gave unwisely."

I continue in my frustration, "When he's drunk later on, it will be all my fault."

Jesus says, "Do you really think he wouldn't find another way to get drunk if you didn't give him the money?"

I look at Him with my mouth open.

"He did something wrong. He lied. He took your money and did something he shouldn't have. But that was *his* money once you gave it to him, and you have no control over what he did with it at that point."

I shake my head in anger.

Jesus says, "Next time, ask to see his car."

"What do you mean, 'next time'? There will never be a next time!"

"Oh, sure there will. This was just a $20 lesson in giving." Jesus smiles from ear to ear. He returns my ice cream cone and pats me on the back with His scarred hand.

I raise my eyebrows.

Jesus continues, "Offer to help him change the tire. If he's telling the truth, you get to help him. If he's spinning a tale, he'll run."

I look at Jesus dumbfounded. He continues, "Really, it applies in any situation. You've got to check his story. Like the journalists say, 'If your mother says she loves you, check it out.' Verifying facts is a normal part of the giving process."

I shrug. "How about you stay with me, and we can figure this out together."

Jesus says, "Sure, this one was small. You'll make more mistakes, but when you do it well, a simple gift of $20 can make all the difference in the world." Jesus reaches out and hugs me warmly, and together we finish the list of errands.

All right, I'll admit it. The story is true, but I embellished it a bit. The truth is, it took me a few days to process what had happened. And, sadly, there was no ice cream involved.

It's awful to get burned. I felt cheated and violated. My joy was stolen. For a while, I was reluctant to give again. Over time, though, Jesus has taught me a number of lessons, and I've loosened up when it comes to want-

> *I'd rather err on the side of generosity than miss out on opportunities to be a blessing.*

ing be the *perfect giver*. I've realized that I'd rather err on the side of generosity with God's resources than be tight-fisted and miss out on opportunities to be a blessing.

TABOO SUBJECTS

What is it about money that has us so tied up in knots? Discussing money is hard, and for many people, it becomes uncomfortable quickly. In the realm of finances, anything we say or do can easily lead to comparison. We show how much money we have by what we wear, what we drive, and the size of our home. We share about our vacations and other expenditures on social media. Even when we are just sharing stories and having fun, the conclusion comes: *He has more than I do*, or *I have more than he does.*

We rarely mean to, but any mention of money with other people often causes us to do some quick mental math. We want to see how we measure up to the other person financially. After comparisons come the inevitable steps of judgment and jealousy. When we find out we are not at the same level as another person, we feel inferior and assume they feel superior to us.

This is nonsense.

Comparison kills gratitude. This is a little phrase I chant to myself over and over again whenever I realize I'm getting a little jealous of what someone else has. Our true value is based on who we are as God's loved people. He made us. He loves us dearly, and He doesn't look at us with a measuring rod that bases our value on our bank accounts. Neither should we. If only we would toss out our sin-tainted way of measuring how we stack up and look at one another the way God sees us, jealousy and insecurity would disappear. It is sad when judgment and envy become a terrible strain on relationships, but it happens instantly and continuously in our conversations every day.

> *Comparison kills gratitude.*

Talking about money makes us uncomfortable. As soon as the subject is broached, people start to squirm in their seats and look for a way out of the conversation. Money is as much of a taboo as sex or religion. Well, we've already talked about money and Jesus, so we might as well talk about sex, right? Wait. No. Fortunately, sex is well beyond the scope of this conversation. Thank God! Look, I know it can be uncomfortable, but we've got to get over our squeamishness about talking about money. But how?

Let me answer that by telling you about my brother John. He's an impressive guy. After graduating from Stanford with a degree in engineering, he has worked and lived in the San Francisco Bay Area for the last twenty-six years. His house is quite modest, and his ability to drive vehicles that cost almost nothing is a tribute to modern technology and God's grace. From his outward appearance, he looks like a man who is content but not thriving financially. What most people do not know is that, when you look behind the financial curtain, you'll see he is truly living like no one else (as Dave Ramsey would say), and it's all by design.

When he was just a few years out of school, married with a wonderful wife and two-year-old daughter, John put together a monthly budget that was incredibly detailed. Of course, as an engineer, he did it on a spreadsheet. Those engineers love their spreadsheets! When he was done, he sat back, thought about the big picture, and asked himself, *Am I doing this right? Does our spending reflect how God wants us to spend the money He has entrusted to us?*

After praying and pondering for a while, he decided to ask Brent, a trusted Christian friend who works in finance, for some advice. John showed Brent his plan and said, "I value your input and would like you to take a look at my personal budget to see if it lines up with a biblical view of money. Let's get together next week and review it."

Who does that? Have you ever heard of someone being this vulnerable with his budget? Brent could have laughed at him. He could have said, "No way!" Gratefully, though, the ensuing conversation was incredibly fruitful. Brent and John included their wives, Mari and Kim, when they met a few days later. Both ladies were from Hawaii, so they talked about the Aloha State to break the ice. "First of all," Brent said, "We are honored that you have trusted us to look at this." He motioned to the page. "I see your income, your investments, and household expenses are all listed. But I have a list of questions before I make any comments."

John nodded.

Brent said, "You have almost nothing for car expenses and a huge budget for vacation. What's up with that?"

"Absolutely! We are content with our vehicle and don't plan to upgrade anytime soon. And, as you know, Kim's family is in Hawaii."

"Right, so is mine!" Mari smiled.

"When we have time off and can travel, we want to be with family. Spending money on relationships is the most important part of our plan. The bulk of our discretionary spending is focused on building relationships."

"Wonderful!" Brent said. "So, it costs a bit more to visit your folks than people whose parents live across the street. I get it, and you're spending these vacation dollars for some very good reasons."

Brent continued. With a calculator in hand, he asked detailed questions about their savings for college and retirement. Over the course of the next hour, they covered every line item on the page. When they reached charitable giving, Brent said, "I understand that you tithe, but you also give quite a bit more. Can you tell me about that?"

Kim said, "We want to be as generous as we can to as many people as we can for as long as we can."

At that point, Brent took off in a detailed conversation like engineers and financial planners enjoy. They concluded that the budget, although constrained from an American Dream standpoint, provided for a significant amount of generosity. This reflected John and Kim's hearts and gave them joy.

Two life-changing events took place at that point. First, Brent and John had broken through the taboo of talking about money and discussed it through the lens of friendship. They have continued to be close friends ever since and have the freedom to talk about finances with each other. Second, John felt validated and pursued his plan of a generous life with confidence. Now, if you were to look at his material possessions many years later, you would never expect his giving platform to be as substantial as it is. John took a bold step and found a way to talk about money with his close friends. In an act of openness and humility, he found the antidote for the taboo of talking about money. Behind the scenes, God is doing amazing things all over the world through the efforts of this humble engineer.

WHERE OUR TREASURE IS

Money occupies an intimate place in our hearts. It is the place where we need to have security. If we have money in the bank, then we usually don't worry about how we are going to pay for our next meal or cover our next bill. Money provides for those things. When we have it, we breathe easier. We feel a sense of freedom as our insecurities are set aside for the moment. When we don't have it, anxiety gains a foothold, our insecurities connect with it, and joy escapes.

Dependence on money normally rules over us. It's true that we need it; when we are ruled by it, however, we don't have freedom in the way Jesus wants us to be free. When we are bound by a dependence on money, it becomes much harder to give it away. Plus, no matter how much we have in this world, there is always a sense that we need more. We see others who have more than we do. We see their comforts and entertainment, and we want what they have. While we strive to have more, we struggle to have enough funds to keep up with the demand. Most people don't live by a budget or know exactly where their money goes. Most people think all their troubles would be over if they just made a little bit more.

I think this might be why God introduced the tithe and calls us to give the first ten percent. When we focus on our own challenges with money and not on God's provision, we continue in our struggle. When our minds are tied up with worry about money, we don't enjoy the freedom God intends for us. We may notice people who have a lot of money and we feel they don't deserve it, didn't work hard for it, or maybe didn't earn it honestly. Then jealousy or anger rears its ugly head, showing that money is still our master in some way. When we feel anger and jealousy toward others, our relationship with Jesus suffers.

I think the taboo around money stems from the fact that we tend to base so much of our security on it. We come to depend on money so much that, when someone starts talking about it, we twitch like someone's touching an exposed nerve. To fix that, we need to hit the reset button. That's what John did when he talked to Brent. He used that conversation to redirect his focus on his *real* source of security, Jesus Christ.

A commitment to serve Jesus changes everything. Jesus starts by saying, "Come and see" (John 1:39). After we are committed to Him, an amazing thing happens: the Holy Spirit indwells us, and our lives begin to resemble Him. His teaching and His love fill our lives as we wholly surrender to Him. This means we have metaphorically placed our lives, our relationships, our activities, and *even our money* at His feet. As Jesus takes His place on the throne of our hearts, money is no longer the master. God assumes authority. This might not happen all at once, but through the process of sanctification, He can take more and more authority over our lives in time. In a sense, He replaces money and becomes our security.

Jesus thinks differently than we do. As we get to know and better understand our amazing God over time, we begin to depend on Him. Teaching about the day-to-day worries of life, He said:

That is why I tell you not to worry about everyday life— whether you have enough food and drink, or enough clothes to wear. Isn't life more than food, and your body more than clothing? Look at the birds. They don't plant or harvest or store food in barns, for your heavenly Father feeds them. And aren't you far more valuable to Him than they are? Can all your worries add a single moment to your life? And why worry about your clothing? Look at the lilies of the field and how they grow. They don't work or make their clothing, yet Solomon in all his glory was not dressed as beautifully as they are. And if God cares so wonderfully for wildflowers that are here today and thrown into the fire tomorrow, He will certainly care for you. Why do you have so little faith? So don't worry about these things, saying, "What will we eat? What will we drink? What will we wear?" These things dominate the thoughts of unbelievers, but your heavenly Father already knows all your needs. Seek the Kingdom of God above all else, and live righteously, and he will give you everything you need. (Matthew 6:25–33)

Imagine walking with Jesus shoulder-to-shoulder, knowing that He cares deeply for you. Imagine that He just spoke those words directly to you, saying, "So don't worry about these things." When we see how He provides for us and we know how valuable we are in His sight, we can feel His love and our trust in Him builds to a point where we can actually rely on God for our daily provisions. As Jesus takes His rightful position in our lives, we release our emotional grip on physical things. We are able to live like they really are His, not ours.

That's a game changer in our financial picture. Think about what Jesus would say as you are making your budget and looking at your financial picture. Would He say, "Maximize your 401(k) and keep plenty in the bank?" Or would He encourage you to give and look you in the eye and say, "I got this." Actually, this is what He said regarding all of this:

Don't store up treasures here on earth, where moths eat them and rust destroys them, and where thieves break in and steal. Store your treasures in heaven, where moths and rust cannot destroy, and thieves do not break in and steal. Wherever your treasure is, there the desires of your heart will also be. (Matthew 6:19–21)

If we actually believe what Jesus is saying, most Americans would have to significantly change their financial picture not to store up for themselves treasure on earth any longer but strive to use money the way God intended. Saving and investing are important, but it can't be *all* we do with our money. We have to learn to store our treasures up in heaven, too.

What does this look like? When money has relinquished its previously held place of power and God sits on the throne of our hearts, we give differently. It means we don't consider giving to be simply an occasional bill in the plate when it is passed on Sunday morning. It also means that giving isn't calculating ten percent and dispersing merely the minimum that is required by the standard of the tithe. It means we give to others the way God gives: *abundantly*! We can't out-give God. With God on the throne, we end up giving more than we would ever imagine! The natural result is that we store up treasure in heaven.

Do you know anybody that prays for an hour a day? I bet you do, although you may not know it. In a culture where people openly proclaim Jesus as their Savior, we would expect many, many people to have lives dedicated to prayer. If you are a part of a church with an active prayer ministry, you are probably surrounded by a number of people who dedicate their lives to communicating with the Lord in their private prayer closet. You might never guess how many hours these faithful men and women spend in prayer. Similarly, it should be common for people to be dedicated to giving and living lives of generosity that would blow people's minds if it were done publicly. In Matthew 6, Jesus talks about giving and prayer in the same breath. Again, I would hope that you know some people who are doing exactly that—although you'd never know.

NORMALIZE GENEROUS GIVING

What if generous giving became a normal extension of our devotion to Jesus Christ? When this happens, our relationship with money would reflect our relationship with our Savior. Every person would become generous in his or her own way, as various and unique as their personalities. Can you even imagine that kind of world—a world filled with creative, outrageous givers? I can.

Anna and I have learned a lot about generosity and experienced great successes with giving over the last few decades. We've also suffered our share of failures that have taught us valuable lessons. Many of us have had bad experiences from giving poorly; this should not deter us from using God's resources generously. Rather, we should press in to see what God has for us as we discover His vast and expansive character. I'm certainly no expert in financial planning, but I have followed the path God laid out for us. I hope that, through some of the experiences we have had, you can see a window into the world that God may have for you through biblical stewardship and generosity.

Looking inside:

1) When have you been burned by giving?

   a. Relive your story of being burned, but this time imagine it with Jesus next to you in the process.

   b. How does that change the picture? What did you learn from Him?

2) Do you know anybody like my brother, John, and his wife, Kim? What emotions did you experience upon reading their story?

3) Kim said, "We want to be as generous to as many people as we can for as long as we can." What would you have to give up in order to accomplish this goal?

4) Think about how your family talked about money as you were growing up. Were the conversations anxious, angry, hopeful, or satisfied?

   a. Did your parents teach you skills in how to handle money?

   b. Do you talk with your parents or your spouse about money now?

   c. How do you prepare your children to handle money?

Taking action:

1) Make a list of some close friends who you can ask to look at your personal financial picture.

   a. Take a risk and have a godly friend look at your budget.

   b. Ask yourself and your friend, *Are we using the money God has entrusted to us the best way?* Be ready to accept constructive comments and be accountable to them.

CHAPTER 3

OUR STORY: GOOSE ISLAND

*Give generously to the poor, not grudgingly, for
the Lord your God will bless you in everything you do.*
Deuteronomy 15:10

Giving was easy when I was a child. At six years old, I prayed
the sinner's prayer with my mother in the backseat of our family Buick. My family practiced tithing and taught me that one shiny
dime from every dollar I earned went into the collection plate. Since
I wasn't really earning much money, it wasn't much of a challenge.
Since we were a military family, my brothers and I never went hungry, but we weren't exactly frolicking in the foothills of financial fortunes, either. I didn't feel any real attachment to giving other than it
being a routine.

Everything changed as I neared the end of my education. My
wife and I lived in La Crosse, Wisconsin, for my arduous years of
graduate study at Gundersen Lutheran Medical Center. Anna and
I had a daughter earlier in my residency program, and, in my final
year, we were expecting our second child. With the long hours in the
hospital occupying most of my time and energy, I hadn't spent the

time or effort necessary to plan the rest of my life. But the graduation date was looming. The time for decision-making was upon us.

I had a number of options before me: a career as a professor, private medical practice, or serving in medical missions full- or part-time. My passion for teaching inclined me to a career in academics. Having spent many years in higher education in a variety of academic environments, it was pretty much all I knew. That being said, my parents had served as missionaries for many years after my father retired from the military. From their example, I had certainly caught the bug. In fact, the hope of being involved in mission work was the reason I went into the medical field. Medical care is a major means of delivering the gospel of Jesus Christ, and I certainly planned to be active in missions in one way or another. I even had a picture of Dr. Gary Parker, a full-time medical missionary, hanging on my office wall. I wasn't that interested in going into private practice, though. I simply didn't see myself doing that. The prospect of earning a large salary bothered me for some reason. When I saw how humbly teachers and missionaries lived, I considered that to be my future. With an extensive education that was completely devoid of any type of financial planning, I had absolutely no idea what I was doing. So there I was, overeducated in my specialty and ready to take the board exam—but a neophyte in so many other areas of life.

I began the process of figuring out where I wanted to go and what I wanted to do. I interviewed at a few practices in larger cities, as well as for fellowship programs to further my education—a path leading to a career in academics. Then I stumbled upon a thriving practice in a smaller town that emphasized all the aspects of patient care I enjoyed. They did plenty of complex cases, routine bread-and-butter work, and a fair amount of pro-bono work benefitting the local community.

I loved this practice. If I were to paint a picture of the practice I would have started myself—had I been so inclined—this would have been it. The Midwestern town was small enough to be friendly, and the staff was first class. What really struck me, though, was that some of the doctors in the practice were active in foreign medical missions. In fact, they had worked into their contracts the ability to take off extended amounts of time for this purpose.

After a couple of interviews with the group, I thought I had found my future. This opportunity seemed right for my family. My only question was, *Is this God's plan for me?* So I prayed. I took time and asked God what He wanted for my life. I fasted and laid out the issues before God. I discussed all the options with Anna, and we sought the Lord's direction together. While I continued to maintain a normal routine day after day, the only issue that occupied my mind was this single major decision. I prayed, but God remained silent.

After weeks without hearing anything from God, I took a rare, precious day off and spent a full Saturday away to think and ask God what I should do. I escaped in my rusty Honda Accord to one of my favorite places a few miles away. I drove through the sloughs of the Mississippi River to a secluded nook known as Goose Island Campground. There, I walked the shores of the river enjoying the magnificent natural beauty and asking God for His guidance. The more I thought it through, the more the job seemed like a perfect fit. As I stood on the bank of the river, I asked Him, *What should I do?* Then I waited.

The God of the universe broke the silence. I heard Him say in my spirit, "Take the job." I knew instantly, without a doubt, that He had spoken.

Insecurity boiled up within me. *Isn't that self-centered and greedy?* I asked.

In that moment, God

> *Beyond that, give everything away.*

impressed something life changing and shocking on my heart. I heard Him say in my spirit, "Here's what you will do. You'll make a base salary for the first two years. This will be your salary for your entire career." I pondered what He could mean by that, but then He continued, "Beyond that, give everything away."

I thought, *What did He just say? Give away everything beyond the starting salary?*

I didn't know what to make of it at first. I had never lived on a significant salary or been in a family with one, so I had no idea what life on a large income looked like. I did have a relationship with the awesome God who was talking to me. I knew that if He told me to do something directly, without ambiguity, it would turn out very good. But God wasn't finished with me yet. As I thought through my financial situation, I was beginning to see the two sides of my financial picture: my take-home pay and God's side.

I asked, *What about retirement savings? Would that come out of the salary or your side?*

I sensed Him reply, "Just as an employer contributes a matching amount to a retirement plan, when the time comes, we will work out similar plan."

I felt like Moses asking God question after question, but I pressed my case, *What about saving for college expenses for the kids?*

"Just like people normally save for their kids, you can do that with your salary."

I continued, *What about the cost of mission trips?*

"Those come from my side."

We continued our conversation about how the process would work. I asked more and more questions, and He patiently answered. He gave me a clear plan for my financial future. I was dumbfounded. Not only had I heard, without a doubt, from the living God what job I should take, but I also knew exactly how to work out my finances for my career.

I spent plenty of time that morning worshiping God and thanking Him for making this plan so clear to me. Whitetail deer silently walked along the edges of the forest as they foraged for food. I enjoyed watching them as I replayed the conversation in my head over and over again. I pulled out a notepad and made notes. I had been expecting to make a list of pros and cons, but with the new information revealed, the process was quite different. On the left side of the page, I drew up a simple budget and laid out how we could manage our home expenses, vehicles, vacations, gas, food, and everything else. I put everything I could think of on the page. It was a lot of detail. On the right side of the page, I drew a box, and inside it, I wrote the word *Giving*. The box was empty.

Giving meant so many different things. Other than giving ten percent of our income to the local church and potentially supporting some missionaries or maybe going on mission trips, I hadn't really thought about it much. I knew nothing. I put a big question mark inside the giving box.

My next challenge was to convey this idea to my bride. I told her about the conversation with God. She knew that I rarely say the words "God said." So, when I recalled the events of the day, she joined with me in commitment to the plan, just as if she had been there on Goose Island alongside me as God rolled out the DeWitt Financial Plan.

We had hope.

We had a future.

And we had a plan.

Looking inside:

1) How have you heard God communicate to you?

    a. Was it through Scripture that jumped out from the pages of the Bible?

    a. Was it through a feeling of peace when you asked Him a question?

    b. Was it through a trusted friend?

    c. Was it by circumstances that lined up just right?

2) Have you ever asked God specifically how to manage the money He has entrusted to you?

Taking action:

1) Describe your own Goose Island experience.

    a. What did God impress upon you?

    b. What have you done with that message?

2) If you haven't had one yet, what's holding you back?

    a. Sketch out a tentative plan to go to your own version of Goose Island.

       i. Where would you go?
      ii. What specific questions would you ask God?

CHAPTER 4

THE FINISH LINE

If you help the poor, you are lending to the Lord—and
He will repay you!

Proverbs 19:17

After I completed my medical training in Wisconsin, our family moved into a modest home and I dove into my new profession. As my first two years as an associate were coming to a close, I wanted to formalize our financial plan, but I hadn't told anybody about the Goose Island experience. In fact, I thought I'd be laughed at or scolded. Who plans to arrange their finances like this? I didn't have a clue what I was doing except to say, "God told me to do it."

I was inspired. I knew what direction to go, but I didn't have much information on the background of biblical stewardship to do it. I had no clue how to implement process; how could we connect the dots between the vision of being generous and the practical steps on how to do it? After a fair amount of research, I found an energetic Christian financial advisor named Rich VanderSande with Smart Stewardship Advisors. I called him and asked about his take on biblical stewardship. His voice lit up over the phone. He explained that he was a Christian financial planner and was thrilled to talk about finances the way Jesus did. When we met in a coffeehouse outside Chicago, I was shocked at his youthful appearance. I expected an older gentleman to match the wisdom I heard on the phone, but

Rich was my age. The professional-looking young man greeted Anna and me warmly.

He taught slowly, since he was just getting to know us. Through a series of specific questions about our values and vision, he introduced some concepts of wealth management, pausing often so I could ask questions. I saw that he was committed to the concept of applying biblical stewardship principles to our financial picture.

Once we were well underway, I could tell that Rich already had a plan in mind for us. He started by quoting Ron Blue, "Everything belongs to God." Using a series of laminated visual aids, he explained that all finances are God's to start with, and He allows us to have stewardship of some of it and trusts us to manage it well. After he flipped through more laminated sheets, I dropped the bomb. I didn't expect to tell anybody about my Goose Island experience because, in my mind, it was pretty radical. Nonetheless, in a moment of disarmed conversation, I told Rich my Goose Island story. He was silent for a moment. I let him know all about our commitment to live on the current salary and give generously out of the increase when it comes.

Rich's astounded expression made me wonder what he was thinking. He said, "It looks like God beat me to the punch!" With his mouth open, he flipped to the next page and showed us the concept of the *finish line*. This is the point where you decide you have enough to live on and can be generous with everything that comes beyond it. Giving away all income beyond the finish line is often seen as a radical idea—but this was Rich's main goal of the meeting, to show us this concept.

We laughed a lot at that point in the meeting—much more than you'd normally expect in a financial planning meeting. His vision and ours lined up perfectly. Anna and I agreed to work out a specific plan with Rich. He took our inventory of personal and professional goals, risk tolerance, and investment knowledge (this part was easy—we had none). Then he came up with a simple plan. He introduced us to the National Christian Foundation (NCF) and helped us open a donor-advised fund.

Anybody can open a donor-advised fund. There is nothing magical about it, but it allowed us to put all financial contributions into a single fund. From this account, we could direct contributions wherever we like as long as they are approved 501(c)(3) organizations. We were in charge of the money, and the accounting for tax purposes was extremely simple.

God had given us direction, then provided Rich, who *just happened* to be in line with our plan and had the tools we needed. All we had to do was follow through, so I met with my local accountant and explained the plan. Graciously, she accepted my unorthodox means of financial management and helped me with everything from banking issues to the ever-present burden of state and federal taxes.

The plan was beautiful in its simplicity, and it worked exactly as we had hoped. We opened our fund and enjoyed regularly logging onto the NCF website to direct funds to support missionaries and various projects in our favorite charities. What happened over the following decade was a series of lessons in faith, giving, and fundraising that I never would have expected without God's direction.

Once I was responsible for managing more of God's resources, I needed instruction. I studied the Bible's teachings on money. I also read as many books on biblical stewardship as I could. I found authorities like Larry Burkett, Randy Alcorn, and Dave Ramsey and devoured what they had to say. I listened to their radio shows and read everything Ron Blue had ever written. I was getting a feel for this new aspect of life along with the challenges that came along with it, yet I still felt alone. I didn't know anybody locally who was doing what we were aspiring to do.

I met with a local friend, Dan Allison. Dan was not only a full-time pastor and church planter, but he also had a full-time job in the financial sector. (Only God would design a job description like that.) He was well connected and knew most of the large donors in the region. I laid out for him my Goose Island experience and what I endeavored to do. I asked, "You know everybody in town, and you know lots of generous people. Do you know anyone who is engaged in what I'm talking about doing?"

Dan furrowed his brow, scratched his head a bit, and said, "Nobody. I've never heard of anybody doing this." That was my lot in life. God had challenged me to live in a way that He had clearly laid out, but Anna and I still felt alone in the adventure.

Rich introduced us to Generous Giving (generousgiving.org), an organization dedicated to teaching biblical generosity. They are unique in that they don't solicit fund requests or allow any to be solicited. They exist solely to facilitate education on the concept of biblical generosity. I read their books and other materials and attended my first Generous Giving conference. Hundreds of people filled a hotel ballroom, and the experience was wonderful. I sat under the teaching of inspirational teachers like David Platt, Mark Batterson, and Ron Blue. I met them, had lunch with some of them, and peppered them with questions. The most inspiring part of the conference took place in the hallways when we met other like-minded individuals who had lived the way I wanted to live. I struck up conversations with people on different stages of their journey of generosity. We all had a variety of experiences, and we all had struggles. We heard a quote from Randy Alcorn who encouraged us to raise our *standard of giving* rather than our *standard of living*.[1] This became a common theme throughout the weekend. Through Generous Giving, I discovered I wasn't alone. Hundreds of others right there at the conference were on the journey with me! All I did was obey and found that there were plenty of others doing the same. I began to think, *This should be normal.*

I continued my quest and dove into more books after the conference. Testimonies of people living generously are tough to find, because most of them do so without boasting about it. With a little digging, I found story after story of people who dedicated their lives to giving. Here are a few of my favorites:

Milton Scott operated a textile mill from age 25 to age 102. He lived simply and, in diligent secrecy, he went about the task of dividing his sizeable earnings among God's interests around the world. He helped smuggle Bibles into Russia before the Iron Curtain fell, equipped preachers in South America, funded Bible translations, and more. Conservative estimates are that he gave 70 to 80 percent of his income. All along, he maintained a lifestyle that barely qualified as middle class.[2]

John Cortines and Gregory Baumer recently graduated from Harvard Business School. They were on the fast track to wealth and success when they changed their focus and set out to live on a modest salary and give away the rest. They tell their story in the excellent book *God and Money*.[3]

In 1951, a young businessman in Los Angeles named Bill Bright and his wife, Vonette, wrote and signed a contract for themselves, surrendering everything they owned to Jesus. Instead of building his business, God gave Bill a vision for an enterprise that would change millions of lives—and the organization Campus Crusade for Christ (now known as Cru) was born. He took no royalties for books or honoraria for speaking engagements. Shortly before his death in 2003, it was noted that millions of dollars had passed through his hands, but he gave all of it away except for a modest annual salary.[4]

In 2015, Sheela Padmanabhan started Ascribe Healthcare Solutions, a medical billing company in Chennai, India. She heard about Jesus for the first time after enduring multiple business challenges and overcoming an abusive marriage. When she dedicated her life to Jesus, generosity sprang forth like a fountain in a desert. She lives on a finish line and gives generously. She has taught others about Jesus Christ and has been open about her charity work. Through this, she has witnessed Muslim and Hindu men and women come to faith in Jesus Christ. They, in turn, have fully sponsored the college education for hundreds of students.[5]

Tom Monaghan, the innovative founder of Domino's Pizza, was a changed man after reading C. S. Lewis's *Mere Christianity*. He rededicated his life to God and, after taking care of the needs of his family, devoted the rest of his life to giving away his wealth in order to help people know Christ. He founded Ave Maria University, to which he has pledged the majority of his remaining resources.[6]

Mike Kendrick runs an investment banking company. He takes his role as a steward seriously, using his platform as a business owner to help fledgling ministries get off the ground. By providing office space and helping them with his administrative gifting, he has assisted dozens of ministries bring their vision to reality.[7]

Donald Rauer had never been generous until he inherited a large sum of money from his uncle. His uncle had set up a foundation with nearly $1 million, and Donald was named the sole trustee. Because of his involvement, abandoned children received medical treatment and starving people were fed. Donald loved hearing all about it. When the fund ran dry, he began transferring money from his own nest egg over to the foundation. Eventually, most of his salary and pension went directly into an operating account for the relief work. By the time he died, Donald's life had been completely devoted to extending compassion to those in need.[8]

When he was twenty years old, Thomas Maclellan surrendered his life to God. He made a covenant with God and, as he developed a successful insurance company, gave generously. Five generations later, his family continues to honor that commitment to God, giving tens of millions of dollars annually to advance God's kingdom through the foundation that bears his name.[9]

These are just a few examples. As you can see from the stories, the people come from every stage of life. Through the miracle of the Internet and YouTube, more and more stories are coming to light all the time. The givers are rich and poor, young and old. Some planned a life of giving from the start, while others fell into generosity by surprise. Some did great things and I would consider them to be giants of the faith, while others served quietly in their own way. But, in each case, God got hold of them in a way that radically changed their hearts—and their bank accounts.

All these stories and more have shown me what I had always prayed to find: I am not alone. Ron Blue once said, "I personally know hundreds of Christians who are serving others by literally giving fortunes away."[10] It shouldn't surprise us when we hear about extraordinary generosity. It should be perfectly normal as an extension of Jesus' love. A faithful reading of Scripture leads us to a relationship with an amazing God who has been extraordinarily generous to us. This shouldn't cause us to ask, *How much should I give?* Rather, it should lead us to the question, *How much do I need to keep?* Once we have that question answered, everything else falls in line.

Of course, I'd be lying if I were to say we've perfectly implemented our plan. Occasionally, over the years, we've gone off course a bit here and there, and God has dealt with us. Through the process of repentance and forgiveness, we've gotten back on track. Your discussion with God may not go the way mine went, but when you engage with Him in dialogue about a financial plan, you'll be able to run with whatever He gives you. God works differently in everybody. Our job is to listen to what He says and obey.

Ron Blue, who has worked with thousands of people in their personal financial plans, said:

The "How much do I really need?" question is a pivotal point in an individual's willingness and ability to exercise generosity. Our earthly resources will always have limits, but we have unlimited choices for how we use them! A finish line can be perceived as a beginning, not an end....Do we need to eat dinner out as often as we do? Do we always need the latest gadgets? What if, instead of satisfying more material temptations and pleasures, we adopted a paradigm shift from fear to faith? …Challenge yourself to be generous in your heart and with your wealth to experience financial freedom and God's richest blessings. Out of this abundance, we believe that you will indeed have *more than enough!*[11]

The more you can do to keep fear from influencing your wallet, the less you risk drifting away from God in your finances. Once the plan is in place, freedom, joy and peace take root and begin to grow.

There are all kinds of new hurdles to overcome in this new adventure. In the next chapter, we'll explore some of the issues we face in the practice of biblical generosity.

Looking inside:

1) Imagine what a finish line might look like in your life.

   a. If you were to cap your salary at a certain level and give everything beyond that, what number could you choose?

   b. What limitations would you be installing in your life? Putting off the new car? Not getting a bigger house?

   c. What benefits would people in need receive because of your sacrifice?

   d. How would Jesus live if He were in America today?

2) How does Jesus measure sacrificial giving?

Taking action:

1) Ask God what changes He would like you to make in your financial picture.

   a. Remember, your story will be different from mine. God loves variety and will be equally creative in how He directs you.

   b. It doesn't matter what stage of life you are in, whether you're just starting out or well into retirement. God is after our hearts and, as we pursue Him, our lives will reflect His generosity.

2) Does your financial advisor or CPA share your biblical convictions about finances and giving?

   a. Who do you have in your life that can help in these areas?

   b. Everyone needs a stewardship coach. Who do you have? You'll find a list of resources for stewardship coaching in Appendix 2.

CHAPTER 5

WHY TALK ABOUT GIVING?

Blessed are those who are generous, because they feed the poor.

Proverbs 22:9

It wouldn't be fair for me to climb up on a mountaintop and declare to the world, "On Goose Island, God told me to give, so you need to do it, too!" However, biblical stewardship is more complex than just saying, "Give ten percent and it's all good." Like most topics in the Bible, there is much more to it, and, of course, there are believers on all sides of the issue. I understand that giving money away is a contentious topic. I have friends who refuse to step foot inside a church because they are offended by the way they "always ask for money." I know folks who are offended because the church has had one scandal after another but still asks for money.

The church has not been perfect throughout history, and all types of inappropriate teaching have been spouted about money over the years. In fact, when I talk with people outside the church about these issues, I usually agree with them when they list the offenses with which the church has been involved. The church is in a precarious position, then, when it comes to education about finances. If a pastor or priest talks about it, they are accused of being money hungry. If they refrain, then the people are uninformed on how God can work in their hearts in this significant aspect of their life.

Yes, the church should teach biblical stewardship with wisdom. We need to hear about money from the pulpit, but it's also a great topic to dive into through a classroom or small group environment, making room for discussion and debate. When we sit down and talk through our financial struggles, share how we've endured painful experiences, and discuss how they could have been handled differently, we can truly make headway through this important topic.

Money is certainly important, but it's not the most important thing in life. Topics of more importance start with understanding your relationship with Jesus Christ—His sacrifice on the cross and then being raised from the dead. Salvation! Absolutely, that's much more important to discuss and is the first and most important issue of all time. As we continue our conversations about Jesus, the Holy Spirit transforms our lives. This leads into relationships between husbands and wives, parents and children, and all kinds of other important issues. Money comes up eventually, but it is significantly further down on the list.

Nobody has ever fallen more in love with Jesus by arguing about tithing or taxes.

When people try to talk about money, the discussion quickly turns into an argument over minutia, such as, "Should I tithe on my gross income or net?" Or perhaps, "The New Testament only talks about giving generously in general, so why should we talk about tithing at all?"

I have plenty of thoughts on these issues, and we'll get to them in a later chapter. I enjoy these conversations and could talk about both topics for hours, but, as far as I'm aware, nobody has ever fallen more in love with Jesus by arguing about tithing or taxes. And generous giving stems from a heart transformed by the love of Jesus in your life. We don't get God's attention with our great lives of giving and thereby convince Him to love us; He's already done the most generous act of all time! He is the creative God who gave us life and gave us the greatest gift of all—His Son, Jesus Christ. Through this very act, God has out-given all of us!

When Jesus is the center of our lives and we are thinking as He does, our default setting changes from *me* to *He*. Instead of being self-focused, we start to love others the way Jesus does. We become the image of Christ for the benefit of others. We find ourselves spending our time differently; we talk with people in a manner of love and gentleness, not selfishness. When we exercise generosity, we are merely reflecting His qualities in our lives.

Certainly, nobody achieves perfection in this life. I'm not saying we should all live in a commune, sit around a campfire, hold hands, and sing *Kumbaya* all the time. But the reality is that Jesus molds our hearts and changes our attitudes toward possessions and money. I think that, if we were to focus on who God really is and fully worship Him, the arguments about tithing gross versus net would fall by the wayside. When we are face to face with the loving, almighty God of the universe and our focus is on Him, our grip on our finances inevitably loosens. At that point, we don't focus on a number like ten percent; we focus on a wonderful, loving God who is everything to us.

But life is complicated. After an experience in which we vow to give everything we can, we wake up the following day, go to the grocery store, and realize how much it costs to support our daily needs. We look at our bank accounts at the end of the month and cringe. Without doing anything malicious or wrong, our focus tends to drop back on ourselves. Our default setting reverts back to *me* instead of *He*, and we tend to close our fists and control our finances with the natural constraints in mind.

That's our nature. It happens in pretty much every area of life. For example, you may vow to be a better spouse, then something happens at a time when you're tired and hungry, and you lash out. It happens. Thank God for the process of forgiveness and redemption. Most of us have tried to do the right thing. We've tried to be generous and things went badly, like my $20 gift to the scammer. But when you lash out at your spouse, you don't throw your marriage out the window, take a vow of celibacy, and go live as a hermit in the woods, right? If that were the case, I would have lived in a Unabomber hut for most of my life! No, the process of forgiveness and reconciliation helps us learn and change our actions. Similarly, God uses our unwise giving experiences to educate us on how to become the wise givers He wants us to be. But that can't happen if we don't actually have a real conversation about giving. We've got to learn how to talk about it.

REASONS TO TALK ABOUT GIVING

If giving is so complex, controversial, and full of failure, why even talk about giving money away at all? Why not just leave the subject alone and concentrate on the more important issues? There are several reasons. Let's break down some of the big ones.

We Aren't Good Givers

The first reason we need to know more about biblical stewardship is because we, as a body of believers, give poorly. New publications come out all the time that detail who gives what. Questionnaires, IRS studies, and lots of data mining reveal what is going on in American churches today. Americans are known as a generous people. However, when experts analyze the giving of those who attend church, the studies consistently say that, of all church attendees, just one-third to one-half give any financial support to their churches. *Any.* Of those who do give something, only three to five percent of church attendees practice tithing. While evangelical Christians may give more on average than most Americans, their giving is still well below a basic tithe. It's alarming that Christians now, in a time of relative prosperity, give a lower percentage of their income per capita than Christians did during the Great Depression.

Similar reports show the gap between what is happening in worldwide ministry *now* and what *could* be possible if 100 percent of the church tithed. What could be done with the financial resources if churchgoers released their tithe to the church? Billions of dollars would flow and countless ministries could be fully funded. With only three to five percent of churchgoers contributing ten percent or more of their income, ministries are starved of the capital they need. As a church body, we should do much better.

> *Christians now, in a time of relative prosperity, give a lower percentage of their income per capita than Christians did during the Great Depression.*

We Can't Ignore Money

Second, money is a central part of our lives; therefore, it cannot be ignored. We use money for all kinds of things. We earn it by working hard, spend it in a variety of ways, save it, and give it. Most of what we do involves money in one way or another.

Jesus said, "Wherever your treasure is, there the desires of your heart will also be" (Matthew 6:21). This means our bank transactions show us where our heart is. When you send a portion of your income to a certain area, your heart goes there. This is certainly a good thing when talking about feeding and caring for your family. It's also a good thing when preparing for retirement and saving wisely, but it quickly gets out of hand when we realize we spend more on hobbies than we do on, say, our children.

Think about this for a minute. Jesus is talking about treasure in Matthew 6; this is right in the middle of Jesus' Sermon on the Mount, His world-class sermon upon which much of His teaching centers.

You can literally study this passage for years and never exhaust the riches of His words. Right in the middle of it is a discussion of money. There's a reason for that. Our relationship with money tells a lot about our relationship with things around us. It sheds light on where our hearts are—whether we like it or not. It speaks volumes about our relationship with God. Money runs in and through almost every other area of our lives. We can't escape it, so we must dig in and explore what the Bible has to say about how to manage it. Through giving, we can draw closer to Jesus.

The Bible Has a Lot to Say about Money

Third, it's important to talk about money because the Bible is absolutely filled with teaching on it. There are 2,350 verses in the Bible about our finances. Jesus talked about money more than He talked about heaven and hell combined. Jesus' conversations with Zacchaeus (Luke 19:1–10), the rich fool (Luke 12:16–21), and the rich young ruler (Luke 18:18–30) all show that how we handle money is one litmus test of our character. It is an index of our spiritual lives. Our stewardship of money and possessions is a big part of who we are as men and women of God.

> *There are 2,350 verses in the Bible about our finances.*

The Bible is an inexhaustible source of information about God's view of financial stewardship. As we deepen our knowledge of Jesus, our amazing Savior, we should also continue to learn what we can from His Word about our money and giving. If it weren't that important, the Bible wouldn't talk about it so much!

Jesus Commands Us to Give

Fourth, Jesus commands us to give. In Matthew 6, we learn a lot about how Jesus views money; however, there is something else intriguing about this passage. Earlier in the same chapter, Jesus also taught about prayer:

> When you pray, don't be like the hypocrites who love to pray publicly on street corners and in the synagogues where everyone can see them. I tell you the truth, that is all the reward they will ever get. But when you pray, go away by yourself, shut the door behind you, and pray to your Father in private. Then your Father, who sees everything, will reward you. (Matthew 6:5–6)

A few breaths later, He gave the first utterance of the Lord's Prayer, Jesus' manifesto on prayer instruction. He continued and taught about fasting as an adjunct to prayer. Just as He commanded us to pray and fast, He commanded us to give in the same passage. In His instruction to live holy lives free from religious hypocrisy, He instructed us to pray without going on the street corners to be seen by others and get credit for looking holy. Similarly, He said to not sound the trumpet to be praised by others when you give. This fuels some churches' hesitancy to discuss money, but there are plenty of ways to talk about money without decrying it on a street corner.

In laying out this instruction, Jesus made the basic assumption that prayer is essential in our relationship with Him. Prayer is a vital element of being a Christ follower. Nobody would argue against that. In the same passage, in the same breath as He's delivering the Sermon on the Mount, He revealed that giving should have the same tone as prayer. We must give. It connects us to God and brings joy. We can't wait to give!

Treasures in Heaven

Fifth, giving is a spiritual act of worship. Dropping a coin in the offering plate as it passes by is as much of a spiritual act as a pastor giving a sermon, praying, or fasting. We have a tendency to ignore the routine parts of a church service as if they were almost meaningless. The songs, prayers, and passing of the plate happen each week in most churches. What we miss is how the simple act of giving is spiritual in nature and an important part of our relationship with God.

After Jesus taught on prayer in Matthew's Gospel, He went on to say:

> Don't store up treasures here on earth, where moths eat them and rust destroys them, and where thieves break in and steal. Store your treasures in heaven, where moths and rust cannot destroy, and thieves do not break in and steal. Wherever your treasure is, there the desires of your heart will also be. (Matthew 6:19–21)

So, are we not to store up treasure for ourselves here on earth? Jesus instructed us instead to lay up treasure in heaven. What does that mean? If we store up in heaven, who benefits from it? Jesus said the treasure we are to lay up in heaven is for *ourselves*! This means your name is on a heavenly bank account. Every deposit you make here has an accounting in heaven stored up for you.

Wait a second, though. Isn't that selfish? As followers of Christ, we are supposed to focus on others, not ourselves, right? Absolutely. We give because of God's love flowing through us with no expectation of reward. Yet the understanding that a gift given *now* results in a deposit we will enjoy in heaven *later* is based completely on faith. Nobody would give money, expecting reward in heaven, without truly believing Jesus' instruction. It's all through *faith*, and that's what Jesus wants for us in the first place. What does it look like on the other side of this life? We can only guess. Could it be increased responsibilities or status in heaven? I have no idea. But we know that we have an all-wise God who wants the best for us, and we can take comfort in knowing His character.

The apostle Paul confirmed the concept of the heavenly bank account in two separate sections of Scripture. First, he encouraged the people in the church of Philippi to be generous. He didn't want them to think he was simply asking them to give *him* a gift, so he clarified, "I don't say this because I want a gift from you. Rather, I want you to receive a reward for your kindness" (Philippians 4:17). I love the clarification. I can even see Paul's hand gestures waving in front of his robe while he's talking. "Hey, I don't want anything, but I do want you guys to be generous and to be rewarded on the other side of heaven for it."

The second time Paul confirmed this concept of the reward is when he was coaching Timothy. At the end of his first letter to his protégé, he wrote to Timothy about how to address the rich in his church. In a wonderful passage, Paul revealed that God makes a promise that, as we pursue generosity, we enter into the life He really wants us to experience. Paul wrote, "By doing this they will be storing up their treasure as a good foundation for the future so that they may experience *true life*" (1 Timothy 6:19, emphasis added). *True life!* We may experience true life by giving! That's quite a statement. It certainly sounds like Paul is saying that, when we enter into a life of generosity, laying up treasure in heaven for ourselves, we are living in faith and living in the manner that God intends for us to live. I think it's fair to say that, when we do that, it is truly life!

But, if it's a bank account in heaven, it will have a value attached to it. When some place large amounts and others simply can't afford to do so, the rich person would have a large value and the poor person, though generous in their own way, would end up with less in their account, right? How does that reconcile with God's character?

Jesus addressed this question, too. In the story of the Widow's Mite (Luke 21:1–4), where Jesus and His disciples were hanging out in the back of the Temple watching people put money in the offering box, Jesus pointed out that a poor widow gave more than the rich did with her modest donation of two copper coins. Jesus views money quite differently than we do and values it accordingly. The donations we make here on earth make deposits in heavenly bank accounts using Jesus' unique valuation system—our hearts. There is no sense comparing one person's donations to another's. It's all about Jesus, not us.

Being generous does not mean God will give back to us on this side of heaven. There are some that teach what is called the *prosperity gospel* that says God wants us all to be wealthy. This teaching says that, if we are generous, He will provide financially for us and we will have riches. They also encourage giving and say that prosperity comes to us when we are generous to others. Some people also encourage us to pray for a withdrawal from our heavenly account, so that we might enjoy our heavenly riches here on earth somehow. This is not what Jesus is saying in Matthew 6. Logically, this philosophy falls apart quickly. According to this teaching, the poor widow who gave everything she had would have become wealthy, and wherever the gospel is taught, there would be no more poverty. Rather, Jesus commended her but gave no indication that her financial status would change. In addition, Jesus later taught that the poor would always be among us (Matthew 26:11).

> *Being generous does not mean God will give back to us on this side of heaven.*

God continues to teach through many circumstances, whether we're living in plenty or living in want. When we have to rely upon Him constantly for our daily needs, this dependency yields a closer relationship. Jesus said we should ask Him, "Give us today the food we need" (Matthew 6:11). He doesn't teach us to say, "Give us a great wealth." People often draw closer to the loving God when their needs are the most oppressive. The instruction to be generous is not a promise of riches but an enlightenment that we are to have a heart like that of our loving God. This is an amazing reality that comes when we enter into the life of generosity that He wants for us. Please understand that the generosity God wants has nothing to do with high-dollar giving; rather, it is living how He desires because of a heart that follows Him.

Jesus made it clear that it's not about the amount given but the heart of the giver that God sees. To demonstrate this point, let me tell you about my friend Hannah. She and her husband had been friends with another couple, Luke and Emily, for many years. One day, Hannah got home after a long day and prepared a typical, simple dinner. As she pulled the meatloaf out of the oven, she received a text informing her that Emily's son was in the emergency room with intractable seizures and was going to be airlifted to a major medical center. Luke stayed home with their other two small children while Emily drove up to be with her son as the medical issues were being addressed.

Hannah immediately stopped what she was doing and lifted Emily and their family up to Jesus in prayer. She quickly finished the meal she was preparing, placed it in a travel dish, hopped in her car, and delivered it to Luke. She made it home just in time for her husband to walk through the door. He greeted her with a kiss and asked what was for dinner. She simply said, "Leftovers," and opened the fridge to see what they might have. She rummaged around and pulled out a few partial dishes while she shared what she had heard about Luke and Emily. Her loving husband joined her in prayer for the family and was pleased that she could help in such a quick and simple way. They were ready to help their friends in their time of need and generosity showed through. I'm sure God was smiling at Hannah's quick willingness to give her own meal away and a deposit was made in Hannah's heavenly account.

Testimonies of generosity from people of meager means abound. For every story of a rich person giving, dozens or even hundreds of people in humble circumstances have stories of generosity just like Hannah's. These stories don't get the same type of attention that higher-dollar gifts may get; however, while they would never make the pages of a newspaper, Jesus knows and cherishes every single one.

Money Reveals the Heart

The sixth reason we need to talk about finances is that money reveals the condition of our hearts. God keeps track of our actions, including our giving. He keeps track of our account balances and encourages us to lay up treasure in heaven by giving here in this life. In the Sermon on the Mount, Jesus continued His teaching on money, "No one can serve two masters. For you will hate one and love the other; you will be devoted to one and despise the other. You cannot serve God and be enslaved to money" (Matthew 6:24). Jesus is clear that our relationship with money is central to our relationship with God. Later in Matthew 6, Jesus says that we should seek Him first and the material things shall be added. Seeking the kingdom of God first is all about knowing and loving Jesus. Really, *all* of this is about Jesus. Money is a tool that He uses to guide our hearts toward him.

God Loves a Cheerful Giver

The seventh (but certainly not the last) reason we need to know more about what the Bible teaches regarding finances is that God loves a cheerful giver. Paul wrote to the church at Corinth, "You must each decide in your heart how much to give. And don't give reluctantly or in response to pressure. 'For God loves a person who gives cheerfully' " (2 Corinthians 9:7). The Bible clearly says God loves those who give *cheerfully*. That's great. When we think about it, the Bible is all about Jesus and His relationship with us. Jesus can be seen woven into the fabric of every story in the Bible all the way from Genesis to Revelation. So, you would think we could find all kinds of passages that describe what God loves, right? Not so much. In fact, there are really only two.

The first Scripture is the 2 Corinthians passage we just read about God loving a cheerful giver. I love that passage. It's comforting to know that God absolutely loves it when we give with a joyful attitude—even in a simple gift like Hannah's meal. The second passage that connects God's love and giving is the most well-known verse of the Bible, John 3:16: "For this is how God loved the world: He gave his one and only Son, so that everyone who believes in him will not perish but have eternal life." Here, John talked about God loving the whole world and giving the most amazing gift He could possibly have given, His *Son*. That's the basis for all of Christianity. It's a big deal, and it's quite clear that God loves the whole world. The interesting thing from a generosity standpoint is the logical progression of the two actions in one sentence. "God loved" is immediately followed by "He gave." So logically, if you love something or someone, you'll give toward them.

I love bow hunting for deer. Sitting in the woods on a cold November day hunting for a big Iowa whitetail buck is something I look forward to all year long. The chance to take home a deer using nothing but a bow and arrow is a thrill for me. I truly enjoy this hobby, so I give toward it. I've spent money on hunting clothes and equipment. I've given my time—often more than my wife would like—but, since it's something I love, I give toward it.

When you love somebody, you give toward him or her. When I asked Anna to marry me, I gave her an engagement ring. It was a symbol of the love and commitment I made to her, and it had a cost associated with it. (For me, however, it wasn't too great a cost. My great-great-grandfather won the diamond in a poker game in Alaska a century ago. I just took the diamond to a jeweler and had it placed in a setting, but you get the point!) The logic here is that giving shows love. Money is only part of the big picture. When you love someone or something, you give. Time, effort, and money are all included in the process of showing love.

When people know God and are grateful for the gift He gave, they can cheerfully be generous with money and possessions. It's a natural reflection of God's love. Giving money cheerfully means that we love and care for the folks receiving the money or items. Giving in this way means the giver's heart resonates with the heart of the recipient. These are all things that make God smile on His people.

What does it look like when we embark on our own personal journey of generosity?

How do we give without being burned?

How do we use finances to impact God's kingdom for good?

Missionaries have a treasure trove of wonderful examples of giving done well and tragic examples of giving without wisdom. In the next few chapters, we'll explore some good and bad examples of well-intentioned giving and discover the value in learning how to *ask* and *give* well.

Looking inside:

1) What does it mean to store up treasure for yourself in heaven?

2) How is it fair that God supplies one person with abundance and another with much less, and then He gives rewards based on giving?

3) What do you think it will look like when Jesus rewards our giving in heaven?

Taking action:

1) What people or events have shaped your view of money?

2) What Bible verse(s) have had the most impact on your beliefs about money?

   a. You may want to do your own Bible study on money, wealth, and giving.

   b. As you reflect upon your beliefs, it's helpful to write out your thoughts in a notebook or journal.

CHAPTER 6

AIR CONDITIONERS

Clean the inside by giving gifts to the poor, and you will be clean all over.

Luke 11:41

Many years ago, I met a fascinating young man named Rico. Born and raised in a poor country, Rico's light-hearted attitude and British accent set him apart from most people I had previously met. We attended the same church and were both leaders of small-group Bible studies. Within a few weeks, Rico and I were getting together every Saturday to walk along a local riverbank. After small talk, it didn't take long for him to ask me directly, "What is God doing in your life today?" I loved it! He continually challenged me to love God and draw near to Him. He asked me lots of questions about my background and what my current challenges were, and I reciprocated.

Rico told me about a young missionary who introduced him to Jesus and gave him a Bible. Rico dove into the new book and approached the missionary every day at 5:00 a.m. with questions. He laughed out loud recalling the social differences between cultures and was thankful for the missionary who got up that early to answer his endless questions and invited him into his house over and over again.

Meanwhile, I was also learning about medical missions. I traveled to faraway countries working with various mission organizations. After each trip, I shared my experiences with Rico. I talked about the heat, the vast areas with so much need, and what we did while we were there. He smiled and nodded, and we went on talking about what Jesus was asking us to do.

At one point I asked him, "Would you like to come on a mission trip sometime?"

He looked at the ground and remembered his childhood. He said, "The trucks with the white people come. They stay for a week and do some things. Then they leave."

I was shocked. I hadn't realized that he had been on the other side of American mission work. He had been the recipient of their "giving." He was gracious to me and encouraged me to go and help, especially providing care in the clinics, but he wanted no part of it himself. I later read an excellent book by Steven Corbett and Brian Fikkert called *When Helping Hurts*. Brian says:

> Many observers, including Steven and I, believe that when North American Christians *do* attempt to alleviate poverty, the methods used often do considerable harm to both the materially poor and the materially non-poor. Our concern is not just that these methods are wasting human, spiritual, financial, and organizational resources but that these methods are actually exacerbating the very problems they are trying to solve.[1]

Sadly, I saw a small example of this type of tragedy unfold before my eyes.

Rico was asked to be a guest speaker at a youth retreat in Michigan. It would be a six-hour drive to get there, and even though there was no compensation, he wanted to go. He had several months to prepare the message and arrange everything he needed to make it an effective weekend. However, it was going to cost him about $200.

Where would the money come from? He had no idea, but he agreed to go and continued to work on his message.

Meanwhile, Rico's church's compassion committee sent one of their members to visit his family. Edna was a retired schoolteacher who lived alone and enjoyed the outing to Rico's house as her main event for the day. She sat with Rico's wife and had coffee in their small living room. The stifling heat was oppressive for the guests, but Rico and his family hardly noticed. To him, the discussion was uneventful and he thought nothing of the visit.

When the church compassion committee met the next time, Edna reported what she had seen and how the heat was insufferable. They decided a great way to show them love was to purchase two window-unit air conditioners for his home. Edna returned with the gift and had coffee with Rico's wife while a young man who accompanied her installed the units in the windows. Later that evening, Rico came home, looked at the air conditioners, and asked, "What's this?"

"People from church came and put those in," she said.

"What?" He was confused. "Why?"

"I have no idea."

"Did you ask for them?"

"No."

"Great!" Rico smiled. "I think we just found the money we need for the youth retreat."

She hugged him, and together they removed the air conditioners and sold them to a friend for $200. God had provided for them!

The following week, walking along the riverbank with coffee in hand, he was floating on air as we talked. "It was the best youth retreat ever!" He said. "The kids responded to the gospel! They want Jesus in their lives. I wish I could have stayed longer." We celebrated together and enjoyed God's provision.

The following Saturday, I was anticipating another challenging and energizing time with my friend. However, when I greeted him, he fumed, "They want their money back!"

"Who?"

"The ladies from the church came and visited again. They saw that we had sold the air conditioners and were upset. Now they are making us pay the church back $400."

I was dumbfounded as he told me the story.

"We didn't want the air conditioners in the first place. They wanted us to have them. Now they are upset that we sold them, and they want their money back."

I shook my head in silence. Eventually I asked, "What are you going to do?"

"I told them I'd pay them $100 a month until they get it all."

I placed my hand on his shoulder as we walked along the shoreline. The morning was more like a funeral than the celebration he had experienced the previous week. "Now I have to write a check to them four months in a row to cover *their* mistake."

HELPING WITHOUT HURTING

There are good ways for a church to give to families, and there are bad ways. A committee with a goal of meeting the needs of the needy in the church has a huge challenge. How do you help without offending the family? How do you help in a way that strengthens people without taking away their dignity or causing them to stay in need? How do you help in a way that builds them up and gets them through a crisis, rather than allowing them to dig deeper into debt?

These challenges are met when people get to know the recipient and treat them as friends rather than just people in need. If Edna had asked me what Rico needed, rather than *assuming* he wanted air conditioners, I could have told them about the mission trip. It would have cost the church $200 instead of $400. They would have met Rico's need with half the cost and built up the relationship. Instead, they made well-meaning (but wrong) assumptions that cost tremendously in terms of anger and resentment.

What Would Jesus Say?

Let's replay this scene with Jesus sitting in the living room with them when the committee member met with Rico's family. Jesus sits comfortably sipping His coffee. Jesus leans in and nudges Edna, "Ask them what they need."

Rico's wife answers, sipping her coffee, "Oh nothing, we are doing very well, thank you."

Jesus nudges once again, "Ask what projects they are doing this summer."

"Oh, we have a big one," Rico's wife answers. "My husband has been invited as the guest speaker on a youth retreat. He works on his message every night when he comes home from work. He's very excited about it."

"That sounds great. When is the retreat?"

"It's coming up in a few weeks. He can't wait."

"Is it here in town?"

"Oh no. He'll have to travel. I think it's a six-hour drive, but he is happy to do it."

"It sounds like an excellent way to earn a little extra money for the summer."

"Oh my," she chuckles. "They aren't going to pay him. He's doing it because he loves the kids."

Edna is shocked. "Then how is he going to cover the cost of the trip?"

"We have no idea," she says. "God will provide. He always does!"

Edna looks at Jesus and smiles. She has just found out how the church can help the young couple. They finish their coffee and enjoy their time together. A week later, Edna meets with the church compassion committee and recommends that they give a check for $400 to Rico's family to help with the youth retreat expenses.

But, who knows? What if Jesus came on the scene after the air conditioners were purchased? He might have used His carpentry skills to help Rico remove them and sell them, hopefully for $250. Then when Edna visited the next time, Jesus would sit on the couch holding a cup of coffee. When they saw that the air conditioners were gone, what would that conversation look like?

Edna says, "I'm so sorry. I didn't expect you to sell those. Why did you sell the air conditioners?"

Awkward pauses are the norm with this type of conversation. I'm sure Jesus would have stroked His perfectly kept beard, waiting for a response.

"We didn't need them, but we needed the money."

Jesus speaks for Edna. "I understand. Once those were in your house, they were yours to do whatever you want with. We didn't own them; you did. What did you do with the money?"

"We used them on a youth retreat," Rico says sheepishly.

"Great," Edna says. "Tell me about it."

Rico then excitedly recounts his experience at the youth retreat and the kids' response to the gospel.

Jesus would have been so happy that He would have jumped up and given them a hug. He probably would have spilled coffee all over Himself in the process.

Sadly, this is not how it had transpired. Painful things were said, a wound was made, and a scar had formed. I wish Jesus had been there in person to try to prevent the rift that came between Rico and Edna that day. Amazingly, Rico was not upset with the church. He didn't blame the pastor. He continued teaching his small group and loving people all over the church, but I wish the whole process been handled more skillfully.

Looking inside:

1) Do you ask Jesus to show you how to help people?

2) Why is it better to wait until a relationship is well established before giving?

Taking action:

1) What is the best process to help someone in need?

2) Some people have made a policy to only give to organizations, rather than to individuals, in order to avoid offenses.

   a. Is this a wise policy?

   b. What type of policy would you form in relation to giving to friends and family?

CHAPTER 7

GIVE YOUR BEST

You will be enriched in every way so that you can always be generous. And when we take your gifts to those who need them, they will thank God.

2 Corinthians 9:11

Willem Charles was born and raised in a small village outside Port-au-Prince, Haiti. This Caribbean island nation is the poorest country in the western hemisphere. Willem grew up with his entire extended family crammed into a tiny house. He learned English as a boy from a missionary's son and became fluent. As an enterprising teenager, he became a serial entrepreneur and formed small businesses that assisted the needs of American missionaries. In 1999, inspired by the love of Jesus, he started Mountain Top Ministries (MTM), which ran a church and a school in his home village of Gramothe.

As MTM gained a foothold in the village, mission teams became one of the major strengths of the ministry. Each team came with a vision and a purpose: paint the preschool, install the steeple, preach at the pastors' conference, and so on. While they were there, team members looked at the village through their own personal lenses. Many times, this led to creative ways to help.

David Jones, an Indiana native, was a friend of MTM from the beginning who regularly traveled to Haiti to help with various projects. He was captivated by Willem's vision. When he saw the children running around barefoot and wearing nothing more than rags, his heart went out to them. Upon returning home from one of his trips, he began gathering donations for Haiti through his church.

David emailed Willem, telling him he could bring a large trailer full of donations. He asked several questions, including:

1. What types of donations do you need?
2. If we collected items in a large trailer, would you be able to get it to the village?

The benevolence of the churches in Indiana had already been well established, and Willem welcomed a trailer full of donations. He replied enthusiastically, "We'd be blessed by your giving. We can rent a truck and bring the trailer up the mountain. Anything you provide will help."

The church in Indiana made announcements from the pulpit and encouraged people to bring all types of donations for Haiti to their facility. They arranged to have everything transported to Gramothe in one huge load. As the donations arrived at the church in Indiana, David began loading a trailer to be shipped to Haiti.

Willem announced to the village that he was bringing a large trailer full of donations from the United States. When people asked what was in the trailer, he just said, "Come, and we'll all find out together." While he did not know the details of what was inside, he knew it was from the same Americans who had been so helpful thus far and was confident it would be quite a load.

David shipped the trailer to Port-au-Prince and traveled there himself to personally receive it. Word traveled quickly when they arrived at the village. Men, women, and children flocked to see the massive gift box, and smiling faces swarmed. Willem unlocked the door, but it wouldn't budge. After considerable effort, he pried it open, and a few boxes fell out as Willem climbed inside.

Items were scattered within the metallic cavern. Willem picked up a box and opened it up, so the crowd could see. He reached in and held two old T-shirts. He flipped through the box, only to find more and more clothing. Much of it was new, but some was riddled with holes. The process plodded on through more bags and boxes. The lumber would be useful, as would a used sewing machine, but most of the toys had broken.

One of the village elders picked up a broken toy and a pair of old shoes and pulled Willem aside. He asked, "This is what they think we are worth? This is *junk*."

Willem tried to explain that many of the quality products had been stolen at the customs office, but there wasn't really much to say.

David walked with Willem back to the house in silence. After a while, Willem looked over to the back porch and saw David leaning over the railing, agonizing over the process that had just taken place. Thousands of dollars had been spent in transporting the trailer. His frustration was palpable. Their next trailer would have to be better.

Willem and David resolved that day to do better; they wanted to meet the needs of the people in the village in a way that honored each of them. They vowed to always give their best. Willem brainstormed over the next few weeks. He dreamed up a wish list of items they would love to have. Rather than seeing only what the village *was* and had *always been*, he envisioned what he wanted it to *become*: a thriving, prosperous town serving as a model for the surrounding villages with resources and support to help them as well. He dreamed big.

They needed electricity. There was no end to the list of new and better things that would be possible once they had constant, reliable electricity. Willem added to his list a new, high-quality, large industrial generator. He knew this would cost $20,000 or more, but this was what it would take to build the village. They also needed better transportation. He and his men needed a pair of all-terrain vehicles (ATVs) to double their productivity. Willem filled out his grand wish list that also included plumbing equipment, tools, and many other quality items.

Willem sent the list to David, who got right to work. With the help of a local contractor, they shared the vision with a generator salesman. He generously provided one at wholesale cost, and amazingly, he gave a second one absolutely free. They contacted an American ATV dealer who had met Willem when he had been visiting the States the prior year. When the dealer heard what Willem was doing in the village and the impact that the ATVs would have on their day-to-day operations, he donated two ATVs.

Over the next several months, they gathered everything on Willem's wish list, filled a trailer, and shipped it. David once again visited when it arrived in Port-au-Prince. When Willem brought the trailer up to the village, hordes of people gathered when the trailer opened. Willem unlatched the doors and announced, "I'm here today to let you know that you are valuable in God's eyes. You are loved because you are God's wonderful children." He let the words hang in the air for a moment, then turned and easily swung open the door.

Stacked from floor to ceiling was their treasure: generators, ATVs, new toilets, water heaters, tools, wiring, and piping. Everything a plumber and electrician would need to get to work was right there. Cheers went up throughout the crowd.

Willem looked at David and whispered, "Give your best!"

The relationship between the giver and the recipient is incredibly important. Every relationship is based on good communication. A gift of old or broken items says, "This is what you are worth to me," but giving a load of over $100,000 of new equipment for a village shouts, "*This* is what you are worth to me!"

Breaking Down the Problem

We may be quick to judge David for collecting only used, old junk in his first donation box, but the responsibility doesn't lie solely at his feet. When David initially asked what was needed, Willem wasn't specific. His nonchalant, general answer actually contributed to the problem. By saying, "Anything will help," Willem failed to provide the direction and leadership necessary. People gave old stuff, junk; however, as Willem and David worked together, they walked through the painful process of learning how to give and how to ask.

Well-meaning benefactors have even saved used tea bags to give to missionaries, wrongly thinking they were helping in a great way. When missionaries receive rare care packages in the mail, they can't wait to see what someone has sent. It's like Christmas for them with all the expectation and joy until they open a box to see nothing but used tea bags. Gross. The message they hear is, "This is what you are worth to me." If you are going to give tea, send a box of new tea bags. Even better, send five dollars and trust them to buy quality tea with it.

I'm not saying every gift must have a price tag on it to prove its newness in order to be acceptable. There are plenty of times when people have given used cars away, and they have been huge blessings for ministries. Used cars have value. Most ministries purchase used vehicles when they need transportation. For me, the depreciation of a vehicle in the first few years is as painful as a herniated disc in my back. But there is a difference between giving something that is gently used versus an item that is about to be thrown away. Purchasing new doesn't always make sense, and since they are looking for used vehicles, a gift of a used vehicle is often a true answer to prayer. Used *socks*, on the other hand? Not so much.

When Willem learned to ask properly and with clarity of vision for specific, quality products, the extent of people's generosity was revealed. They were a giving people who offered to help, and they did exactly as they were asked. They were able to give generously because he clarified what he needed and shared the vision.

JESUS ENTERS THE PICTURE

Imagine that same story once again. This time, as Willem brings the first trailer to the village, Jesus is standing there with him. Jesus' skilled carpenter's hands help him get the trailer door open when it gets stuck and consoles him when the giving goes badly. When they hear the Haitian elder say, "Is this what they think I'm worth?" guilt and shame become the major emotions mixed into the experience. Jesus coaches Willem: "I'm a big God, so ask big!"

Now, picture Jesus helping Willem put together his wish list. As Jesus and Willem walk through the village, Jesus whispers, "Imagine if we had an industrial generator at the back of the church." Willem thinks about this and dreams of endless possibilities. Jesus says, "Remember when somebody mentioned how an ATV could tackle this mountain? Let's ask for two of them."

Jesus is sitting next to David at the computer when he opens the email and sees the wish list. David's first thought is, *Are you kidding me? How can we get all this stuff? It will cost a fortune!* But Jesus gently guides him, "Why don't you call some of your friends?"

Before David has the chance to ask his friends, Jesus helps people connect to Willem's vision, and He prompts their generosity. Jesus gets busy all around the small Indiana towns. By the time David calls and inquires about the equipment, the salesmen have already met with Jesus and are ready to step out in uncommon generosity. The soil of their hearts has been tilled, and the seeds have been planted and watered.

When they finally make it to the second revealing, Jesus stands at the back of the crowd. He looks all around the village, well aware of exactly how each piece of equipment will transform the rudimentary village into a thriving town. He applauds with the crowd as the new equipment is carefully placed on the ground. The edges of His white robe are caked with mud as He dances with the Haitians. They celebrate the benevolence and the hope of what is to come for their village.

The relationships among all the parties involved are exceptionally important in giving. Friendship among the giver, the recipient, and Jesus grows as communication improves and giving is done well. As believers, we are called to love our neighbors. We can communicate love simply by giving our best!

Looking inside:

1) Why is it important that Jesus leads both the giver and the recipient?

2) Describe when Jesus has guided you in a small gift that made a significant impact for someone.

Taking action:

1) Make a list of some organizations you love. Before asking how you can help them, what do you need to know?

   a. What do they need?

   b. What are they asking for help with?

   c. How can your skills and resources help with their needs?

2) When have you had to be reminded to give your best?

CHAPTER 8

ASKING WELL

Ask, using my name, and you will receive, and you will have abundant joy.

John 16:24

In the past few chapters, we have examined the heart of the giver and giving in general, but this is only half the equation. Logically, if there is a godly, generous giver who is learning how to give well, there must also be a God-ordained recipient. The process of learning to ask well is equally complex. Let's shift gears a bit and discuss the mindset of the recipient.

How many soup kitchens, after-school mentoring programs, schools, and churches are limited by financial restrictions? They see their God-given vision and want to do everything they can, but they look at the bank account and sigh. "If only we had the funds, we could do more!" It's humbling to admit that we need other people's money to accomplish our vision.

Does anybody *enjoy* asking for money? Fundraising has a negative connotation in many circles. Is it a pleasant thing to come to another person with your hat in hand, groveling for other people to provide you with money? Even if the money is for a good purpose, we don't enjoy the process of asking. We generally shy away from it; yet asking for money seems to be a necessary evil that goes along with ministry. Some call it *draising* because there is no *fun* in *fundraising*.

Or is there? Could we be wrong about this?

God has many names in the Bible. One of them is Jehovah-Jireh. This literally means God the Provider. This name first appears in Genesis 22:14 as God provides Abraham with a ram to be sacrificed in place of his son Isaac. He is the one who provides for us. The name Jehovah-Jireh is also used in a number of other instances in the Bible.[1]

God owns everything. If you looked over the countryside of a cattle ranch and counted out one thousand hills, you'd find that He owned every single cow (Psalm 50:10). He has access to all the money that exists, yet He calls people to action and tells them to raise funds. He wants us to partner with others, and in doing so, He makes it so we need to ask well.

If asking for money is part of doing the ministry God has asked you to do, then by definition, fundraising is a God-given command. Therefore, since God has commanded it, nobody should be ashamed of it at all. We should run *toward* it, rather than away from it. Asking with your hat in hand, groveling, and being ashamed is not at all what God wants. Being embarrassed that you have to ask has no place in a proper donor-recipient relationship. When we ask in the right way, with the right heart, and in proper relationships with our friends whom we call donors, then we are in complete obedience to God the Provider!

RETHINKING FUNDRAISING

To help demonstrate the heart of the recipient, let me tell you about my friend Dennis. Dennis Rima works as the development director for the Clarity Clinic, a local pregnancy clinic that provides pregnancy services and options for girls and women who are considering abortion. I recently had lunch with him because I was pursuing his perspective on generosity. He loves to talk about the babies the clinic has saved. I started with the simple question "How do you like your job?"

He replied, "Have I told you how I got this job? It's a great story. I've probably told you before."

I shook my head and took a bite of my sandwich.

"I was the principal at a private school in a nearby town for years. I loved my job, and the thirty-minute commute was no problem until my wife was diagnosed with breast cancer. Our kids were three, ten, and eleven at the time, and our schedules became impossible to manage with my wife's chemotherapy treatment. I had to take on some of her normal roles when she wasn't feeling well and help pick up the kids after school. Plus, I got to manage the home and take care of my wife. Because the travel back and forth was incredibly burdensome, I started looking for job opportunities in town."

He continued, "Meanwhile, the Clarity Clinic was undergoing its own challenges, and they desperately needed a new executive leader and fundraiser. Jay Schiesl was the director of the board at the time. He told me that, as he was praying, God had laid on his heart, 'Don't do anything until you talk to Dennis Rima.' "

I took another bite of my sandwich while he ramped up his story. "That's when I got a phone call out of the blue from Jay, who asked me if I would consider becoming the development director of the Clarity Clinic. Nothing could have been further from my mind. I had been a teacher, coach, and then a principal. I knew what I was good at and was well established in my career. Why would I consider taking this job at all?"

He let the question hang in the air for a second before continuing, "But Jay was a friend. Out of courtesy, I reluctantly interviewed with the board with no intention of taking the job. They were talking about the mission of saving babies, and I sat quietly thinking, *Okay, I'll listen.* I loved the mission and the vision, but I really didn't want a job that required me to ask for money."

Dennis paused his story for a moment and said, "I've always taken time to pray over big decisions in my life. I know when God is directing me by the peace I feel in response to my questions." He smiled and said, "I know it's not very quantitative, but having peace over a situation has consistently been how God communicates with me, so I listen."

I wondered aloud, "I would imagine the job was quite different from anything you'd ever done before."

He agreed. "Absolutely. After the interview, I prayed about it for a week. Though my mind was telling me to look elsewhere, my heart was completely at peace with the clinic. My wife was concerned about me taking a job where I had to ask people for money, but I had complete peace." He laughed out loud as he recalled, "I even tried to make myself anxious whenever I considered the job. It didn't have any effect! I just had peace! That's how I knew it was from God. I accepted the job in June 2007 and started a month later."

When Dennis sat down at his new desk and got to work, he sorted through the clinic's financial situation. He discovered that the center was $140,000 in debt, with multiple ongoing expenses, including contracts for expensive ads. The more devastating news was that the previously broad donor base had dried up, and there was no current income. None. He met with an accountant and went over the spreadsheets. "I learned that the center was only two months from being forced to close its doors. That's when the Lord rose up in me and I said, 'Closing the doors is not an option.' "

He said, "I was shocked by our position. If it weren't for the peace I had and knowing that God had brought me there, I would have run away from the position. While we continued to see women and girls in the clinic and had some great success stories, the reality was that we were in trouble."

Dennis sprang into action. He stopped all nonessential contracts and operated with a skeleton staff. He negotiated extended payment on outstanding debts and held a fundraising banquet. Without the cash to hire a speaker for the event, Dennis took to the podium himself.

I interjected, "I was there at that fundraiser. You did a great job."

He smiled. "Thanks. When I got in front of the small crowd of loving supporters, I didn't ask people for money. I asked them to save a life. I wasn't asking for myself; it was for the babies we would save. I told them that every penny we bring in is a penny towards saving a life!"

They raised $112,000 that first banquet, which provided the clinic a little breathing room. Since then, they've paid off the debts, added staff, and grown the number of babies saved. The integrity of the clinic was slowly re-established, and the donor base has grown. They have been able to move to a better location and expand the number of babies they save each month.

Dennis said, "When you calculate how much it takes to run our clinic and how many lives we save, we know that it takes $1,200 to save a baby. I no longer ask for people to help in general ways. I ask them to save a baby. I ask for $1,200!"

People responded.

Churches that had been donating $4,000 per year jumped to $12,000 with the new message. But Dennis wasn't finished. "I tell people, if the very best you can do is $5, then give $5, and you'll be a blessing. If you can do more, then please do." He was literally coming out of his chair with excitement as he spoke. "If you do your best, I promise you that we will not stop. We will not quit. We will not give up until every one of God's precious children is protected in the womb."

I felt like pulling out my wallet right then and there at the restaurant, even though we were just talking about Dennis's job. His passion for the mission of the Clarity Clinic poured out of him like a river of life. He continued his story and talked about how donations doubled quickly.

I asked, "Do you ever feel ashamed about asking people for money?"

"Are you kidding?" he laughed. "I have nothing to be ashamed about!" I felt silly for even asking the question.

He dove right in. "I'm not asking for myself. I know what the money is for. In Proverbs 6:16–19, the Bible lists six or seven things that God hates. One of those is the shedding of innocent blood. God *hates* the shedding of innocent blood! That's what we are out there trying to prevent with every fiber of our being! Asking people to help us save those kids doesn't bother me a bit."

I was at a loss for words. My notebook still had a litany of questions, but at that point in the conversation, I was dumbstruck. His soup was cold and untouched, but he continued, "I'm the representative for the unborn child. The babies are screaming in the womb, 'Help me! I want to live!' I feel I am representing them or speaking for them because they cannot be heard in the womb. But my voice *can* be heard!"

He paused for a moment. His eyes lit up and he continued, "You know, the next Mother Teresa is out there in a womb somewhere. My job is to save her. How could I possibly be ashamed of that?" He let that sink in and finally took the first spoonful of his soup. I marveled at his passion. He continued, "There's nothing better in my job than when a girl chooses life, takes her pregnancy to term, and has the baby. Then, several months later, she brings that wonderful baby into the clinic, and we all get to celebrate and hold the precious one in our arms!"

Dennis was unapologetic. "Asking for money is as much of a spiritual exercise as giving a sermon, praying, or serving a meal to the homeless. Asking for money is not only necessary, but it is an opportunity for people to join with us in saving a life."

I asked, "Does your donor base fluctuate with the ups and downs of the economy?"

He smiled. "Not really. In fact, even during the 2008 recession, our donations never wavered."

Dennis continued with more details, and I felt like he had poured out his heart. As we finished our lunch, I wiped a few crumbs off the table as I got up to leave, and he left me with a parting thought: "The heart of a minister is to ask people to join in the mission. When people join us, they are partnering in saving babies! Asking for money is nothing more than asking for other people to join in the mission with us. When people join in the mission, I get to have new friends. Our donor base is really a base of friends, and when people join with us in the mission, babies are saved."

My head was spinning. I had just experienced a man sharing his heart, and it just so happened that Dennis's heart and his job were aligned in a way that fulfills him like nothing I've ever seen. Through his career at the clinic, he has never slowed down, made apologies, or wavered. His entire story has been about one thing: God sent him on a mission to save babies, and he's running with it.

I was blessed and inspired to be on the other side of the table.

HOW WE ASK MATTERS

When I returned to my office after my lunch with Dennis, I tried to quantify what had just happened. I wanted to boil Dennis's story down into bullet points for the type-A personalities among us. Here are the six things I came up with, which are partly based on the summary points from Henri Nouwen's great book *A Spirituality of Fundraising.*

First, asking for money is a spiritual act. Just as much as anything else God asks us to do, asking for funds is simply being obedient; we should do it with eagerness and passion, expecting a divine response. Jesus talks about giving in the same breath as prayer and fasting in His Sermon on the Mount. As we've seen, giving is a spiritual act that is expected of us, something we do in obedience to Him. Asking for money is no less spiritual and no less important than the giving itself. Thus, we should work at it and prepare for our fundraising events with diligence and excellence.

Second, asking for money is asking people to join with you in the mission God has set out for you. This is no place for embarrassment. There is no shame in sharing your calling. Rather, sharing your vision reveals your heart. In Dennis's case, he boiled it down to saving babies. When we ask for money, we are inviting people into spiritual communion saying, "Come, get to know us and join in our effort." This allows people to enter into a new relationship with us *and* with their wealth. When they put their wealth toward our vision, both sides are connected in the mission.

Make no mistake: fundraising takes enormous effort. It's not an easy task to clarify the vision and run with it over and over again. Inviting people to join the mission is hard work. There's also the hassle of dealing with endless questions and suggestions on how you should do your ministry differently. Some people are hard to get along with or just plain strange, but all of this is part of ministry. When you share your vision and what the funds will do, you are blessed, and those who join your mission are blessed as well.

Third, we should ask with a planned approach. Dennis was literally sitting down at the table with his soup, but inside, he was jumping around! I could feel it. The energy and passion he displayed showed that he was proud of the clinic, the work that they did, and that the money they raised would go to saving lives. Too many times, I've seen people afraid of broaching the subject of money; they'll share the vision but never actually get to the *ask*.

I once went shopping for a car and was kicking tires when a salesman approached me and started chatting. He asked about where I was from and what I did for a living. He started telling stories from his own life, and I really enjoyed listening to him. We talked for over an hour, and during the process, I refocused on the car shopping several times, only to be drawn into more conversation about other things. I had done my research; I knew what I wanted to buy and what price I was willing to pay. I was ready to pull the trigger, but the salesman was more interested in his own discourse than making a sale. He never asked me if I wanted to buy the car! I eventually went to another dealer and came home with a car. The salesman's conversation lacked focus, and he had lost sight of the objective of selling a car. I'm sure that the salesman ended up finding a new job before too long.

In the process of fundraising, making the *ask* is expected. It should be done skillfully and in a way that joins two people together in partnership on a mission together.

Fourth, if you come back from a fundraising activity and feel drained and somehow tainted—as if you've engaged in unspiritual activity—something is wrong. Asking others to join in your mission should build you up rather than drain you. Over the years, Anna and I have met with lots of ministries and heard countless presentations about plans and dreams. When we meet for lunch as prospective donors, we are excited about what mission we can join.

A few years ago, we had lunch with a young man who was fundraising for his upcoming year of internship with a student ministry in a church. I was expecting a jovial college minister who would share the gospel of Jesus Christ with countless students. I was hoping to hear stories of people who had heard the gospel and had turned their hearts toward Jesus. Instead, he described the daily tasks he would be doing, meetings he would attend, and paperwork that it involved. He said, "I'm sorry to bother you with this, but I will have expenses and was hoping you could help with that." I've never had a more disappointing meeting in my life! You can certainly guess how his lack of excitement translated into our level of joining in his mission (i.e., donations).

Conversely, my experience with Dennis was thrilling for me. I was energized by the contagious passion he exuded. As we departed, I asked how he felt, and he said he felt great. He looked like he was ready to be shot out of a cannon as he headed back to his office.

Fifth, our response to the *ask* should be based on God's direction rather than on the flamboyance of the presentation. Some development directors are skilled salesmen who can put on quite a show, and people raise their hands out of pure adrenaline. The flashier the show, the more people give. God would much rather engage each of us personally as we hear His voice speaking to our hearts. Sometimes, God uses a skilled speaker to do so, but other times, He can inspire us to give in spite of a poor *ask*. Our focus should be on God, not the excitement of the moment.

Finally, fundraising results in forging new relationships, offering a new brotherhood, new sisterhood, and a new way of belonging. Ministries have something to offer: friendship, prayer, peace, and love. People who are givers need relationships with people in ministry. They often have needs that can only be met through counseling and prayer. This is a valuable resource, and many ministers are willing to make themselves available to sustain them.

My friend Brian Pendleton, one of the people we support, works as a prayer minister in the International House of Prayer of Kansas City (IHOPKC). His daily work is fairly complex. He does a lot of training and administrative tasks, and I like to joke with Brian that he prays for a living. Along with most staff members at IHOPKC, he commits at least twenty hours a week to prayer in the large IHOPKC prayer room. I often rely on Brian for additional prayer support when I have needs or struggles. Pastors and ministers of all types should routinely offer prayer, counseling, and other types of support to each of their donors as part of the partnership. When this is done well, the relationship grows stronger, and both sides are blessed.

Jesus wants us to go on mission for Him. Often that mission requires money, and we are to ask for it in the proper manner with wisdom. Fundraising is all about sharing the mission and having people join with you. When your passion shows through, the stories you tell

> *When you ask in a confident, strategic manner, people will gladly join.*

reveal your heart for what God has called you to. And, when you ask in a confident, strategic manner, people will gladly join.

Looking inside:

1) Did Dennis's passion for the unborn change when he talked about the mission of the Clarity Clinic versus when he talked about money?

2) Do you think Dennis would talk about money differently with a $10 donor than he would with a $100,000 donor?

3) What's the difference between *donating to a project* and *partnering with an organization*?

4) Starting with prayer and Bible reading, make a list of spiritual activities that people engage in.

   a. Is it true that giving money is a spiritual act?

   b. Is it true that asking for money is a spiritual act?

Taking action:

1) Money and power often go together. There is also a real relationship between power and a sense of self-worth.

   a. How do we use money to control people or events?

   b. How do we use money to make things happen the way you want them?

   c. Do any of these questions make you uncomfortable? Why?

2) Where does prayer come into the process of fundraising?

CHAPTER 9

I THOUGHT IT WAS JUST 10 PERCENT

*They share freely and give generously to those in need.
Their good deeds will be remembered forever. They will
have influence and honor.*

Psalm 112:9

Why can't it be simple? If we just set a rule for giving and keep to it, then there's no argument and everyone knows exactly what to do. Why didn't Jesus simply lay down the law and mandate the ten percent tithe? As we explore the concept of the tithe a bit, I think we'll find that it's much more of an issue of the heart than it is of calculating ten percent and earning "holy points" in God's book by checking the box marked *Tithing*. If you search the Bible for a percentage that is pleasing to God, whether you want to call it obedience or just cheerful giving, you'll find one number: ten percent.

One of the landmark episodes where this came into play was the book of Genesis, early in the life of Jacob. Before he was renamed Israel and became the father of the twelve tribes, he had an encounter with God in a dream of a stairway to heaven. He saw angels ascending and descending on it and heard God declare, "I am the LORD, the God of your grandfather Abraham, and the God of your father,

Isaac. The ground you are lying on belongs to you. I am giving it to you and your descendants. Your descendants will be as numerous as the dust of the earth" (Genesis 28:13–14).

This is one of the all-time most significant promises of all the awesome things God has ever said and done for people. Jacob viewed the place where he had been sleeping as the very gateway to heaven. He did not take it lightly. Jacob was thrilled that he was in the presence of God. He made an offering by pouring oil over a rock that he set up as a memorial and made this vow:

> If God will indeed be with me and protect me on this journey, and if He will provide me with food and clothing, and if I return safely to my father's home, then the LORD will certainly be my God. And this memorial pillar I have set up will become a place for worshiping God, and I will present to God a tenth of everything He gives me. (Genesis 28:20–22)

When God promised to pour out a blessing, it's interesting that Jacob's response was to promise to practice tithing. Blessing is reciprocated with blessing. Note also that God did not ask for the tithe before He gave the blessing.

The concept of the tithe is depicted forty-four different times in the Bible: thirty-five times in twenty-six verses in the Old Testament and nine times in six verses in the New Testament (New Living Translation). Not only that, but four of those New Testament verses directly quote Old Testament references. This consistent giving requirement observed in the Old Testament makes us think there's something about ten percent that God has decided is appropriate. Maybe He knows something about the way we are wired, and this amount is the precise measure that will keep our hearts from drifting as our wealth fluctuates.

GIVING MORE THAN ENOUGH

Let me tell you a story. Pastor Jack led a typical, modern suburban church. There was nothing unusual about Jack or the church until one Sunday when he stepped behind the pulpit, and everyone in the church could actually *see* Jesus standing next to him! When Jesus placed His hand on Jack's shoulder and smiled, Jack's face began shining so brightly that the people recoiled at the sight! Jack saw fear in the congregation and eventually stepped off the stage for a minute and donned a veil before he returned to the podium. He talked about Jesus while Jesus stood right there next to him. God's glory became so real that the people were soon on their knees, overcome with the power and glory of the living God. The presence of Jesus simply overwhelmed the small church. The next week, as he took his comfortable place behind the pulpit, Jesus was there with him again. Jack started recording the services, and his sermons went viral through social media.

The scene repeated itself week after week. Pastor Jack and Jesus were both there. Jack's face shone with brilliance, and he had to wear the veil every time he graced the pulpit. As word got out about Jesus' presence, the church building was filled to capacity. Everyone came with the expectation of seeing Jesus. They were never disappointed. Jack's sermons were the same as what he'd always preached—he taught about God's love and shared personal stories that brought the gospel message to life. With Jesus there loving on people, there were tears in every eye. People were dedicating their lives to Jesus every day. Baptisms became so frequent that they had to hold separate services every week just to hear testimonies and perform the baptisms. The celebrations in the church were amazing!

Jack then had the idea of building a large, full-time worship center. This would be a beautiful facility where people could worship day and night. He had plans drawn up, ordered construction bids, and set a budget. He even displayed a model of the campus in the foyer. This was a large project, far greater than anything the small church had ever tried to tackle. The vision of the new center was clear, and Jack spoke about the new building from the pulpit. With Jesus standing right there next to Him, he asked for donations. People responded with a unified heart and open wallets. Many people who had been coming to the church for years gave freely. Generosity also flowed from those who had been there only a few weeks, far beyond what was expected. People gave cash, deeds to real estate, and even stocks. Online donations poured in from all over the world. The giving skyrocketed!

Before long, the giving surpassed the multimillion-dollar budget. Jack looked at Jesus and asked, "What do we do?"

Jesus simply responded, "Tell them to stop. There are plenty of other places to give."

The following Sunday morning, Jack and Jesus stood at the pulpit. After giving his normal plea to draw near to God and love Jesus, Jack said, "May I have your attention please? We have enough to build the worship center. Please stop giving."

Jesus smiled. The generosity shown through His people had given Him great joy. Jack continued, "There are other places to direct your generosity." He went on to talk about a few ministries that they partnered with and encouraged people to shift their giving to those other causes. Can you imagine it? When people clearly saw the glory of God and were presented with a mighty project to give toward, they become radically generous.

The Biblical Version

You probably think this story is 100 percent fiction. Believe it or not, it really happened—but it's not exactly modern. You could call it *modernized historical fiction* because this episode of generous giving actually happened in Israel's history. The scene is recorded in Exodus 34—36. The Israelite people had been brought out of Egypt and through the Red Sea by a series of incredible miracles. They had not only been freed from slavery, but the Egyptians actually gave them gold and silver. Israel plundered Egypt as they left the country.

The Israelites had seen God do amazing things. They had gone from being slaves to being wealthy, free people overnight.

Moses continued meeting with God on a regular basis after they were freed, and the people saw Moses' face shine because he had been in God's presence. It was like a fluorescent bulb, and the people were really freaked out by him. Moses had to put a veil over his face to make the people feel better about approaching him. It was at this point that Moses cast the vision to the people of Israel for building the tabernacle of God. It was to be a place to worship Almighty God. Moses was given clear instructions on how to build the tabernacle. It would be beautiful with gold ornaments and fine linen decorations, yet nothing was possible without the paraphernalia needed to build. They couldn't exactly run out to the hardware store to buy lumber, so Moses put out a specific call to the general assembly and asked for donations:

> Then Moses said to the whole community of Israel, "This is what the LORD has commanded: Take a sacred offering for the LORD. Let those with generous hearts present the following gifts to the LORD: gold, silver, and bronze; blue, purple, and scarlet thread; fine linen and goat hair for cloth; tanned ram skins and fine goatskin leather; acacia wood; olive oil for the lamps; spices for the anointing oil and the fragrant incense; onyx stones, and other gemstones to be set in the ephod and the priest's chest piece." (Exodus 35:4–9)

That is a very specific *ask*! Moses and his lustrous appearance inspired the people. As they were amazed by God's glory, generosity flowed throughout the camp.

The story continues:

> So the whole community of Israel left Moses and returned to their tents. All whose hearts were stirred and whose spirits were moved came and brought their sacred offerings to the LORD. They brought all the materials needed for the

Tabernacle, for the performance of its rituals, and for the sacred garments. Both men and women came, all whose hearts were willing. They brought to the LORD their offerings of gold—brooches, earrings, rings from their fingers, and necklaces. They presented gold objects of every kind as a special offering to the LORD. All those who owned the following items willingly brought them: blue, purple, and scarlet thread; fine linen and goat hair for cloth; and tanned ram skins and fine goatskin leather. And all who had silver and bronze objects gave them as a sacred offering to the LORD. And those who had acacia wood brought it for use in the project. All the women who were skilled in sewing and spinning prepared blue, purple, and scarlet thread, and fine linen cloth. All the women who were willing used their skills to spin the goat hair into yarn. The leaders brought onyx stones and the special gemstones to be set in the ephod and the priest's chestpiece. They also brought spices and olive oil for the light, the anointing oil, and the fragrant incense. So the people of Israel—every man and woman who was eager to help in the work the Lord had given them through Moses— brought their gifts and gave them freely to the LORD. (Exodus 35:20–29)

Do you think people were pulling out their calculators at this point and figuring their ten percent? Were they concerned about whether their gift was tax deductible or not? Nonsense! They were giving because they had seen the glory of God and were responding in love. They were inspired because they had been in the presence of God and had experienced His glory. They were in love with their God. When we know the presence of God and see His glory, personal financial goals and tax issues seem trivial in comparison.

Moses didn't put his hand into the coffers and take some for himself; he handed everything over to the workers. The passage explains:

Moses gave them the materials donated by the people of Israel as sacred offerings for the completion of the sanctuary. But the people continued to bring additional gifts each morning. Finally the craftsmen who were working on the sanctuary left their work. They went to Moses and reported, "The people have given more than enough materials to complete the job the LORD has commanded us to do!" So Moses gave the command, and this message was sent throughout the camp: "Men and women, don't prepare any more gifts for the sanctuary. We have enough!" So the people stopped bringing their sacred offerings. Their contributions were more than enough to complete the whole project. (Exodus 36:3–7)

That was a special time in the history of the Israelite nation. Truly a glimpse of heaven when the fever of generosity had spread far and wide to the point where the builders looked at the piles of gold, fine linens, and every material that they needed and said, "This is too much!" Moses had to go directly to the people and ask them to *stop* giving.

How many churches wish that they had this problem? What would the church look like today if we saw our pastors' faces shining when they stood with Jesus behind the pulpit? Can this happen again?

When Moses asked with a shining face, their hearts were softened, and they gave so much that Moses had to tell them to stop. Here is the greatest point: there was no reference to the tithe in this biblical passage at all. None! This is the heart of biblical generosity, and we see it in the Old Testament clearly without any poetry or imagery that can be misconstrued. God is after our hearts, and money *reveals* the heart. When God has our hearts, money flows naturally. Every penny we spend tells a tale about our relationship with Him.

THE TITHE IN SCRIPTURE

Money is a big deal to God. There is plenty of instruction in the early portions of the law in the Old Testament that point out what the

Israelites were to do with their giving. The taxes and offerings were spelled out in excruciating detail, and warnings and condemnation came when people didn't follow the law.

Test God

The prophet Malachi scolded the nation of Israel for not giving their tithes. Through Malachi, God proclaimed:

> Bring all the tithes into the storehouse so there will be enough food in my Temple. If you do ... I will open the windows of heaven for you. I will pour out a blessing so great you won't have enough room to take it in! Try it! Put me to the test! (Malachi 3:10)

Nowhere else in the Bible does it say we are to even consider *testing* God. In fact, we are told *not* to put the Lord our God to the test (Deuteronomy 6:16). This is what Jesus quoted to Satan himself when He was tempted (Matthew 4:5–7). Putting God to the test, for the majority of the Bible, is off limits. But here, with regards to finances, God is making a challenge to us. Throwing down the gauntlet, He says, "Come on, try me." Why did God do this? Why did He challenge us to test Him in giving?

We tend to connect our money to our security, so by giving to Him, we declare that our security is in Him, not our money. He has promised to pour out so much blessing that there will not be room enough to store it. He is talking in agricultural terms—how much blessing could a farmer receive before running out of room to store it? That's something the Israelites could imagine. They could picture barns full of harvest and selling crops they can't store. This is a normal desire. It's a unique challenge to put God to the test and start giving to see what He will do.

Jesus and the Tithe

Jesus talked about money a lot, but He rarely talked about the tithe. The main passage we see is actually an indictment against the religious leaders of the day: "What sorrow awaits you Pharisees! For you are careful to tithe even the tiniest income from your herb gardens, but you ignore justice and the love of God. You should tithe, yes, but do not neglect the more important things" (Luke 11:42). Jesus only mentions the tithe once (the scene is repeated in Matthew 23:23), but the reference is crystal clear. Surprisingly, though, there are plenty of Bible teachers who claim Jesus never talked about the tithe at all. It is easy to find contemporary articles that say the tithe is only mentioned in the Old Testament. I would encourage those teachers to pick up the Bible and read the verses from Luke 11 and Matthew 23. Jesus was clear when He said, "You should tithe." But the emphasis was on the heart, not on the calculation of ten percent.

BUDGETING THE TITHE

Let's get serious for a minute. If you know that God's called you to tithe but you simply refuse to do it, is that a problem? I think so, yes. What if we've never been taught about giving this way? What if we've never heard about the tithe or anything about giving? In this case, we are not in disobedience. Scripture says, "Remember, it is sin to know what you ought to do and then not do it" (James 4:17). Therefore, if we have been taught but are not practicing generosity starting with a tithe, then we are in disobedience. We, as Christians, need to take the Word of God seriously and apply His principles in our lives. We need to obey.

Giving ten percent is a good start and a discipline that all Christians should practice, just like praying every day. As we see how Jesus loves and provides for us, extending beyond that baseline of ten percent is the natural outgrowth of our love for Him. Something amazing happens when we switch the question from "How much should I *give*?" to "How much do I need to *keep*?"

Making It a Priority

Giving involves mathematics. We have to add or subtract somewhere along the line, and the accountants use their precious spreadsheets. There's always potential for giving to become a lifeless formula or a legalistic duty, but that's not how biblical, Jesus-inspired giving should work. God doesn't need our money. Rather, He wants our hearts. When our generosity is from the heart as an extension of our love for Jesus, giving becomes a priority.

This would make giving the top priority in your monthly budget, putting it above mortgage, food, car, and all the other expenses. If you wait until that provision has dwindled and been reduced by life's obligations, then generosity is squelched. That's just how priorities work. If you prioritize your giving, then everything else will take its proper place in line behind God's work.

Imagine having a large dinner party for an honored guest. You've cleaned your house and even scrubbed the baseboards. Every countertop sparkles and smells like pine. You've set out your best china on your finest tablecloth. The meal is ready to serve: beef Wellington with mushroom duxelles served with madeira sauce. On the side are bacon-wrapped asparagus, oven-roasted tomatoes, and mashed potato puffs. It will be served with bottles of Cheval Blanc 1947 and topped off with baked Alaska.

You are engaging in all this effort for a large group to honor your guest, Jesus Christ of Nazareth. He's right there in the room with you. You guide Him to the head of the table and, when everyone has convened, ask Him to say grace. You and your helpers walk around the table serving the dishes. The food is served skillfully and not a drop spills. A dozen guests receive their portions and compliments echo all across the room. Jesus is served last. You get ready to serve His meal but then …

Oops! The food and wine run out just before you get to Him, so you run to the refrigerator, scrape together yesterday's mac and cheese, and find a sippy cup half-full of Kool-Aid. It doesn't matter how well you arrange the food on His plate or how large His portion is, Jesus is not honored at the table. His food is the worst. Of course, Jesus could turn the Kool-Aid into Merlot, but that's not the point. The point is we want to honor Him with our best!

We want to honor God with our firstfruits, not our leftovers.

I would hope we would never let this happen, but that's exactly what we do to Him in our spending when we don't prioritize our giving to Him first. Putting our tithe first in the budget makes it a priority. We want to honor God with our firstfruits, not our leftovers.

Be Spontaneous

I love to be spontaneous! My favorite type of vacation starts with hopping into a car and seeing where the road takes me. Granted, this worked much better when I was young and single and rarely works out well with a wife and three kids to consider. Planning is better. Now we do all our vacation arrangements ahead of time, and we have a course mapped out. We still include enough buffer time, which lets us change things up now and again on a whim. My wife and I often change our course midstream in a vacation, but this is only possible because we make allowances for it. Yes, I've become boring. I even have to *plan* my spontaneity.

Spontaneous giving is similar. You can do it only when you've built in margins that allow for it. If there is room in your giving plan for an unexpected gift, then you have a fantastic opportunity to help when you are prompted. (We will talk more about being intentional with your giving in the next chapter.) Beyond the giving we can predict, unique opportunities show up all the time. God brings people into our lives who are blessings to us, and we can sometimes be a blessing to them. This comes easily when you have a strategy. Part of the giving plan allows a buffer zone, so we can go off course when God brings that special person into your life!

Evangelism Through Tithing

Talking about tithing can also be used to share your faith in Jesus Christ. In June 2017, NFL quarterback Derek Carr made headlines after signing the most lucrative contract in NFL history, to the tune of $125 million for five years. In an interview, he simply said, "The first thing I'll do is pay my tithe like I have since I was in college."[1] This declaration made headlines and drew attention across the planet. He used the attention to refer people back to Jesus Christ and continued his normal Twitter posts of Bible verses and evangelistic posts. It wasn't bragging, nor anything unusual for him; rather, it was a continuation of proper stewardship that he had done for years.

When we got married, Anna and I started by committing to give ten percent. Ten years later, the Goose Island experience was possible because we had been faithful with our commitment. It's quite possible that Derek will give above and beyond his tithe, too, but we will most likely never know if that happens. It's his private stewardship of his resources that God has entrusted to him, and, quite frankly, it's none of our business.

PROGRESSIVE GIVING

Whether you're ready to give a full ten percent or not, I recommend picking a number and starting there. Percentage giving is a great place to start. It's the best way to create benchmarks and get a handle on an otherwise intangible decision-making process. It's also a great foundation on which to build a growing lifestyle of giving. As long as we are taking one breath after the next, God intends for our faith to be growing. Our faith and actions go hand in hand (James 2:24), and He wants us to be gradually transformed into the likeness of Christ. He does not want us to plateau or go back to our lower level of faithfulness from previous years. That's the nature of the relationship. He wants more of us, a steady growth toward Christlikeness.

Progressive giving is increasing the amount we give year after year. If we are giving ten percent, then we ask God how much more He wants us to give the next year. God will communicate with us; it might be subtle, but He will let us know what He wants. It might be eleven percent, fifteen percent, or something altogether different, like a certain dollar amount as a giving goal. (We'll talk more about goals in a later chapter.) God wants us to progress in our relationship with Him in all areas of life: prayer, our relationships with our spouse and children, our career—everything! Our giving is no different. He wants us to grow in our giving. Test Him on this; that's not my suggestion—it's His!

Spoiler alert! As you commit your money to God, a couple of things will happen. Once you make a sincere commitment to giving, don't be surprised when the car breaks down, the basement floods, or the dishwasher stops working (or all three). Stepping out in faith doesn't happen in a vacuum or without the commitment being tested. God will often allow the adversary to throw a curve ball to shake us off our game. Our job is to refocus on Him and stay true to the commitment. This is normal; it's part of life. This is when we stay on our knees and depend upon our amazing God for provision in spite of every challenge that comes our way.

When you commit to giving a percentage of your income, it's simple, clean, and clear. The numbers don't lie. Ten percent is still ten percent whether you feel confident God will meet your needs or not. You have a target you can aim at regardless of how your emotions fluctuate. He has promised to throw open the gates to His blessings. So think of it this way: what type of blessing do you want? Are you satisfied with a blessing on one percent of your income, or do you want a blessing on ten percent—or more? Do you want as much of the blessing that our heavenly Father can give?

SO, WHAT ABOUT 10 PERCENT?

So, where does that leave the tithe?

God knew what He was doing when He instituted the concept of the tithe. In Jesus' own words, He encouraged us to tithe. Ten percent is a great baseline for all of us. In addition, when God shows up, we can be generous in thousands of creative ways. Through committing to tithing, we experience the wonders of being a part of God's community. When we willingly and lovingly share what God has given us, our hearts are lifted, and we enjoy being the generous body of Christ that He meant us to be.

Jesus said, "It is more blessed to give than to receive" (Acts 20:35). When our hearts are focused on God, I think mathematics goes by the wayside in light of understanding God's heart for us—just like it did for the Israelites when they gave so much that Moses had to tell them to stop giving. In this light, generosity takes on a new meaning.

Looking inside:

1) Have you ever had a worship experience where you felt Jesus so near to you that nothing else in the world mattered, when you knew He was taking care of you?

   a. What would it be like if an entire church body felt that way when the call is made to raise funds for something?

   b. How would that type of giving affect the worship experience for each individual?

2) What is our attitude toward taxes if we are giving with a heart of worship?

   a. What's more important: the donation or the ability to deduct that gift on your tax returns?

   b. It goes without saying that we should be wise with our money and pay only what is required in taxes, but are there times when you give without worrying about tax deductibility of the gift?

3) What was Jesus talking about when He encouraged the Pharisees but accused them of neglecting the more important aspects of the law?

4) Should church membership require tithing?

Taking action:

1) Write out a position statement on the tithe based on what Jesus said about it.

2) Write out what progressive giving as an act of worship could look like in your long-term financial plan.

CHAPTER 10

THE GIVING PORTFOLIO

The generous will prosper; those who refresh others will themselves be refreshed.

Proverbs 11:25

"Your portfolio includes the Vanguard 500 Index Fund with a return of 7.14 percent." Bernie, my retirement specialist, spoke with vigor and eloquence as I sat at a conference table in my office. "If you look further down the page, you'll see how the Causeway Emerging Markets Fund outperformed at 15.92 percent." He continued talking about the performance of the T. Rowe Price 2030 and, of course, Morningstar ratings. My eyes began to glaze over as my attention span surpassed its limit.

Bernie started the meeting sharing a few stories about his kids, and I did the same. We enjoyed a donut and a few laughs together. About five minutes into the meeting, everything changed when he started talking about portfolios. He droned on about investments and maximizing growth. Bernie could list his favorite top ten or twenty funds right off the top of his head, and he loves to talk about them for as long as anybody will listen. After an hour of bleary-eyed head nodding, we agreed that the economy wasn't predictable, and we would have to watch it closely.

As you develop a collection of investments, you form your own individualized investment portfolio. It may include real estate, stocks, or other investments based on your interests, assessment of value, and personal risk tolerance. There is plenty of attention to building healthy financial portfolios in the finance industry. Money grows in these portfolios, but these funds rarely result in someone being educated, served a hot meal, or provided access to clean water. Nobody hears about the love of Jesus Christ through this money. There is another portfolio, though, that few people discuss: your *giving portfolio*. This is the collection of people and organizations that you invest in for the kingdom of God.

What are the top five organizations you would love to see succeed? How about the top twenty? That part is easy. It's easy to support great organizations we know about. But how do we investigate to *really* get to know them? Like Bernie, we should dig a little deeper into each one and start asking questions, such as:

- In what locations are they operating?

- Can you recite their vision, mission, values, and goals?

- What are their strengths and weaknesses?

- What was the focal point in their most recent newsletter?

- If you invest in them, what kind of direct benefit will you see?

- How do they measure success?

- What do you learn from reading their last few years of 990 forms, the federal tax form required of tax-exempt nonprofits?

Are you feeling overwhelmed? So was I, at first—but we had to push through the challenge. As we really started to understand God's plan for generosity, we discovered that the best giving is not done randomly and scattered by the wind but with wisdom. Our giving should be strategic, prioritized, and planned.

> *Our giving should be strategic, prioritized, and planned.*

When we discovered the responsibility of being a steward of God's resources, Anna and I found ourselves working hard in the process of finding out where we would give and where we wouldn't. In the process, we developed our giving portfolio. I'll share some of our experiences and how our giving portfolio evolved, but first let's take a step back and talk a little more about investments.

Recently, my twenty-year-old daughter opened a retirement account. She wisely decided to put some of her summer earnings away in an IRA. Her account will have a variety of rather small investments. She hopes to add to it and watch it grow over the years. Similarly, a giving portfolio starts small, and as we give specifically and strategically, it has the capacity to grow over time. Nevertheless, it has to start somewhere, usually with small gifts. As we demonstrate faithfulness, God brings more. When managed well, such a portfolio can grow into a mighty force for good.

In the Parable of the Talents (Matthew 25:14–30), Jesus tells the story of a man who challenged three men with resources before going away on a long trip. While the master was away, two of the servants put the money to work in investments, and the other hid the money in the ground. When the master returned, he wanted to see what each servant had done with the capital he had provided. The servant who hid his money was scolded harshly while the servants who had invested well were commended. The master said, "Well done, my good and faithful servant. You have been faithful in handling this small amount, so now I will give you many more responsibilities. Let's celebrate together!" (Matthew 25:23). God wants us to be faithful in small things first. Later, as we demonstrate responsibility, He may choose to trust us with more.

ROLLING UP OUR SLEEVES

When Anna and I committed to the Goose Island plan, we needed a strategy. This was much more than just deciding to give our money away. We needed to be more specific. At our earlier meeting with our financial planner, Rich VanderSande, we celebrated when he showed us we had backed into the concept of the finish line. This conversation was by no means over at that point. With his flip chart, he helped us discover how our family's portfolio of giving could take shape.

Rich asked, "Who really owns your money?"

I answered, "God does."

Rich nodded and paraphrased 1 Corinthians 6:19–20: "God has full ownership of me and everything entrusted to me."

I smiled, happy that I had gotten the question right.

He continued, "Who manages it?"

I was pretty confident on this one, too. "We do."

Rich flipped a laminated page and showed an image that said, "I will open the windows of heaven for you. I will pour out a blessing so great you won't have enough room to take it in! Try it! Put me to the test" (Malachi 3:10). We talked about the concept of the tithe for a while and decided to set aside the firstfruits, starting with at least ten percent of all I receive, treating it as holy and belonging exclusively to the Lord.

I looked at my beautiful bride and waited for her response. She said, "We are fine with this. I remember watching my mother write out the first check of the month as their personal tithe check when I was a little girl. She pinned it to the board in the kitchen then gave it at church. I'm on board with that."

Rich dug a bit deeper with his next question, "What is money for?"

I blurted out, "A new red Ferrari."

Anna laughed. Then she looked at me and said, "Focus, Andy!"

Rich shook his head at my lame attempt at humor.

I smirked and said, "Finances provide security for our family and enable us to help others."

Rich nodded, "So, if we give, how do we choose who to give to and who to say no to?"

At this point, I had nothing but a blank expression on my face. I looked at Anna, who was equally expressionless. Rich said, "When we declare what we don't know, the quest for learning begins."

Anna and I both laughed.

From there, the conversation switched gears a little bit. Rich wanted us to start thinking about our passions.

He continued, "What topic can keep you talking late into the night?"

I didn't hesitate, "Medical missions." I told a few stories about medical missions, and it didn't take Rich long to jot down *Missions* on his notepad.

Anna chimed in, "Church plants." Rich raised an eyebrow, and she told stories of young churches that we'd been involved with and how much they have meant to her. She also talked about Cru (formerly Campus Crusade for Christ) and how college ministries are pivotal in the development of many students' lives.

Rich explained that people can be passionate about plenty of causes. Here's a partial list:

- Evangelism—church planting, Scripture translation, missions

- Culture—the arts, media, history preservation

- Justice—efforts to end modern slavery and oppression, abused and neglected children

- Church—the local ministry of your house of worship

- Support—prayer, stewardship ministries

- Growth—discipleship, youth ministry, counseling

- Education—elementary, high school, trade school, college

- Poverty—food, clean water, shelter, medical care

God doesn't give *everybody* a passion for *everything*. Most likely, each of us is drawn in one way or another. We will feel especially called to give to the area of our passion. This is how God designed us. Just like we are most fulfilled when we serve within our passion and gift-ing, we feel God's joy most when our giving lines up with our passions.

We continued the conversation for quite a while, and Rich added to his notepad a few passions that we held dear. He summarized our interests. I leaned over and peeked at what he had written:

- Medical missions

- Spreading the gospel of Jesus Christ

- Ministries that equip people for service

I nodded, amazed at how he took a convoluted conversation and boiled down the passions that burned in our hearts into three simple bullet points.

Rich said, "What would make you give toward a specific organization?"

"If we knew them well," I said. "Trust is the biggest thing."

"How do you get to trust an organization?"

"Trust builds slowly but leaves quickly," I replied. "When we've been with them for a while and know the people in charge, we see how they work and how they handle their resources."

Our conversation went on for quite a while. Rich asked about our children. They were young at the time, but we wanted to include them in our journey of generosity. We had no idea how to do what we set out to do, but as we did it, we wanted our kids on the journey with us every step along the way.

Rich eventually got to the end of his questions, and I felt like we had just opened a can of worms with no way of sorting through it all. He flipped through his notes and then started writing on a new page. He had helped us discover where our passions lie. We shared with him where we wanted to give through the process he had guided us through, and he had even discovered what criteria we would use to do so. He started to turn the notepad around, but before he did, he took it back and smiled at me. He scrawled a title on the top— "DeWitt Family Stewardship Philosophy"—then handed it to me.

DeWitt Family
Stewardship Philosophy

We are stewards of the resources that God has entrusted to us. Our philosophy comes from biblical teaching and the effect Jesus Christ has had in our lives (Deuteronomy 8:18; 2 Corinthians 9:11).

We recognize that affluence affords us the following:

1) The ability to help others
2) Financial security
3) Time to pursue personal spiritual development
4) The ability to help ministries grow and thrive

We will demonstrate our family financial values by how we lead our daily lives and by involving our children in charitable giving and service. Our family will become involved in a church where we will encourage the spiritual community to work in order to learn the biblical use of money.

Of all the general categories of charitable organizations, we are most interested in:

1) Medical missions
2) Evangelism
3) Ministries that equip people for service

When it comes to deciding which charitable ministries we will support, we will evaluate organizations using the following filters:

1) Accountable, with regular financial reporting
2) Efficient, with minimal administrative costs
3) Trustworthy, with a good reputation
4) Effective, with emphasis in evangelism
5) Consistent, with effective leadership

This was not a paper to be filed away and forgotten. I read it and re-read it every day for a few weeks. I asked God if this was what He wanted us to do with the money He would allow us to steward. Over the course of the next few months, it settled into a solid, firmly established philosophy for developing a giving portfolio.

When the money became available, Anna and I got to work. As opportunities came up for us to be involved and we thought about giving to one organization or another, we referred to our philosophy over and over again. This mission statement provided vision and direction for our giving. It helped us develop a portfolio of organizations that we gave toward.

A family mission statement helps guide the direction of our commitments. Some people have used the concept of a mission statement to provide guidance for how they volunteer. People who are service oriented and say yes to everything tend to get burned out and frustrated. A clear volunteer philosophy will help differentiate what type of projects to volunteer for and what to graciously decline. Our stewardship philosophy is our mission statement specifically regarding finances.

Rich walked Anna and me through this process, and we have been very happy with the direction our stewardship philosophy provides. However, this is only one way of doing this. A family or group of friends can unite to form a *giving circle,* in which all the members share their passions and focus their giving dollars together. Picture investment clubs where people pool their dollars and investment knowledge to invest in businesses. Giving circles employ the same concept, but they invest in ministries that further the kingdom of God. Some people focus on one ministry and others on another, and some may just come along for the ride of learning about giving. Combining their efforts and their dollars, the group can make a significant impact. A giving circle is a fantastic way to unite friends and family around a common theme. As Helen Keller said, "Alone we can do so little, together we can do so much."[1]

In the next chapter, we'll explore the process of research a bit more and examine how it works (and how it sometimes doesn't).

Looking inside:

1) What are your passions?

   a. What subjects can you talk about until the wee hours of the morning?

   b. What kind of experiences have you had volunteering in ministries you were passionate about?

2) Have you ever given money to an organization that you weren't excited about because of guilt or pressure? How does that compare to giving in areas you are passionate about?

Taking action:

1) Draft your personal family stewardship philosophy.

   a. Capture your beliefs about money, your view of generosity, and what causes you are passionate about supporting.

   b. Use this as the foundational building block for all your future giving.

   c. It can be as short and simple as a single paragraph, or it may take shape as a multi-page composition.

   d. Consider doing this as a part of a group, such as your family or giving circle.

2) The stewardship philosophy is a living document and can change as your family, beliefs, passions, and/or resources evolve.

CHAPTER 11

DATING, HIRING, AND FIRING NONPROFITS

Give, and you will receive. Your gift will return to you in full—pressed down, shaken together to make room for more, running over, and poured into your lap. The amount you give will determine the amount you get back.

Luke 6:38

Anna and I started small. A friend introduced us to a young couple, Steve and Jill Schmidt. Steve was working as a budding staff member at the college ministry Cru in Minneapolis. We enjoyed a lunch with them, enjoyed hearing about his ministry, and committed to partnering with him. Later, we met another great young man serving for Navigators and, a few months after that, a couple at the International House of Prayer of Kansas City (IHOPKC). Each of these men and women proved to be faithful workers in their respective fields and stayed in close communication through their newsletters and emails.

Simultaneously, we were looking into medical mission organizations. When we traveled with a medical team, we didn't just go on

111

a trip, help out in the clinic, and take a bunch of pictures. Rather, we treated it like we were dating the organization. We wanted to build long-term relationships with people in missions even though our involvement was through short-term mission trips.

Somewhere along the way, we knew we would need to have a DTR—a *define the relationship* talk. So, when we planned a relationship with an organization, we could be strategic at the outset and find out if our giving goals lined up with their ministry in action. The bottom-line question was, "Do we want to partner with them?"

Anna told me this takes all the romance out of a relationship. She would rather just let it happen, and we would simply fall in love! In a perfect world, she'd be right. I can imagine it happening that way: a couple's eyes meet across the room at a wedding and they talk late into the night. A few months later, they get married. They have kids and then "happily ever after" happens. Right? Well, I've never read a romance novel in my life, but I would guess that they don't go like that.

By looking into the organizations ahead of time, I was hoping we could avoid a lot of pain and suffering. Like any dating relationship, we started with the basics: by stalking them. No, not really. Anna tells me that stalking is the ultimate romance killer. However, we *do* need to get as much information as possible ahead of time by looking at their website and talking with people in the organization. This is a bit like hiding in the bushes but a lot more socially acceptable.

You can find out many things from the website. What is their purpose? What is the organization's reason for existence? Is their mission compelling, clear, and well defined? What makes it unique? Is there a sense of accountability? There are also some questions you can't answer until you've been involved: Are they innovative? Do they plan for contingencies, or are they always in crisis mode? How do they approach decision-making? How do they raise funds?

At some point, a first date has to take place. Often a short-term mission trip is a perfect date. It can be serving in some other way; regardless, throughout the experience, we need to ask about the character of the leaders. Are they passionate or half-hearted? Are the staff members high-energy? Do they have a unified sense of purpose?

I went on three dates doing various types of trips with mission organizations in Africa, Nicaragua, and Colombia. I came home with hundreds of pictures, some great experiences, and major conclusions about what I loved and some things that made me shake my head. The first date answered a lot of questions.

Meanwhile, Anna went on a date with an organization in Haiti. They didn't have any work available in my specialty, so I stayed home, thinking my efforts would be best served elsewhere. However, when she got home, I could tell she loved much more than the experience of working in a foreign country; she loved the mission, vision, values, and goals of the organization.

It was time for some more detailed questions: Do they have a history of success? If it's a new ministry, does the founder exhibit the qualities that are important to me? Do they have measurable objectives to gauge their effectiveness? What goals have they reached lately? With those questions in mind, I joined her on a trip.

This type of relationship can't be realized through simply talking about the ministry and trolling the Internet. It takes work. When the ministry's goals line up with your passion, it doesn't feel like work; it's simply finding out more about something you love—just like dating!

We enjoyed getting to know our friends in Haiti, but we knew we wanted to know more about the organization as a whole. After long days in the clinic, I stayed up late with the founders and listened to their stories. I celebrated with them in their successes and mourned their losses. I asked questions about their long-term ministry goals, such as, "Is the organization tracking progress and working toward clearly defined goals?" Then came the big one, "Are lives being changed?" By the time I wanted to ask that question, I already knew the answer. The church, school, and clinic were well known for the help that they were providing. We learned their fundraising, expenses, ministry model, and goals; and we could see where we might fit in it. By the time we were able to wrap our minds around all the facets of the organization, we realized that we were *already* in it with both feet.

The ultimate litmus test of any ministry is the question, *is it bearing fruit*? No matter how well intended or well run a charity or its programs are, those don't mean much if they aren't creating true change in the lives of those they serve. It's crucial to remember this question is about quality, not quantity. Some nonprofits are not called to reach large numbers of people, yet they have tremendous positive impact. As Jesus taught in Luke 15, it's just as important to go after the one lost sheep as the ninety-nine others who are with the shepherd.

> *The ultimate litmus test of any ministry is the question, is it bearing fruit?*

FIRING A MISSIONARY

Through a long process, we started filling our giving portfolio with other types of ministries that came our way. We said yes to some and redirected others to folks who might be more lined up with their passions.

A few years into our plan, Jerry, a family friend, asked us to support his son during an internship year at a church. We looked over his résumé, his plan for ministry, what he wanted to learn, and how he wanted to serve. When we went to lunch, we listened to his vision and asked a few questions. While it wasn't the best sales pitch, we decided to support him at an introductory level. For the first few months, we saw his reports of what God was doing in his ministry and in his life, but then a month went by without anything. Then another. Soon it had been a long time since we had heard anything at all from him.

Anna and I discussed what we should do about it. We had committed to helping for one year, so we continued in our promise. We planned to conclude our commitment at the end of the twelve months but also considered what it would take for him to re-establish the relationship. He would have to make a significant transition from the limited communication and show something different from what we had been seeing. It was up to him. But what about our relationship with Jerry? Would he be offended if we didn't continue to support his son? I was a little worried that this could put a wedge in our friendship.

At the end of the year, we concluded our giving. We had been consistent with our promise and had supported him, but we had no idea what he had done with our investment. We had no obligation to commit further, so we didn't. I don't know everything God was doing in the young man's life through the internship, but I'm confident that, from a donor's small part in the process, I did what God wanted me to do. As it turned out, our relationship with our friend Jerry remained strong.

GIVE THEM A RAISE

Meanwhile, our friend Steve was doing great things at Cru. He had been in constant contact with us with reports of what he was doing and how God had moved in his ministry. When we realized he was doing so well, we discovered the concept of giving missionaries a raise!

At a regular job, employees are paid based on the value they bring the company. They normally start low and increase over time based on performance. The value they bring to the company is reflected in their wages. Similarly, the base level of support that we started with for our missionary friends needed to be re-evaluated. Steve was doing great work. The base level was no longer how we saw him as a minister. He had increased value; he was consistently bringing students to know the love of Jesus, and the gospel was being spread through his work. That value translated into an increase in his support. So we gave him a raise, and we loved it!

My brother John said it perfectly. "I get a raise every year, both for the cost of living and based on my performance at my job. Because I give a *percentage* of my income, my church gets a raise when I do. So, why wouldn't the missionaries I support get one? I've been supporting some of them for decades. The monthly support I started with doesn't cover what it used to; they need a cost of living increase, too."

We started with a portfolio of missionaries who were all supported at the same level. Over the years, we've added more, given some raises, and taken a few off the list. We try not to support more people than we will actually pray for on a regular basis. While it would be great to have a list of many people all over the world doing all types of ministries, if the list isn't personal and we can't remember who the people are and what they are doing, then we don't have a real relationship. By praying with expectation for each of the missionaries on a regular basis, we know their needs, pray for them, and look forward to their next newsletter with updates. Some people might have the capacity to pray for dozens of missionaries in addition to their family and friends; my preference is to keep the list smaller. That way, I can recite their names and keep abreast of their current situations.

> *We try not to support more people than we will actually pray for on a regular basis.*

The most interesting thing is that the level of support varies widely. The new kids who are just getting their feet wet are at the base level, but the experienced ministers who are key players in their role at an organization receive support commensurate with not only our relationship but also how well they add value to their organization.

BEING A CYRUS SUPPORTER

As our portfolio grew, we discovered the concept of being a Cyrus supporter. Cyrus was a Persian king in the Bible. He gave the modern-day equivalent of billions of dollars to rebuild the city of Jerusalem (Ezra 1:1–4). Today, Cyrus supporters are the faithful, regular, monthly donors that missionaries and organizations can depend on for a significant part of their support. Cyrus supporters give them ongoing financial stability, enabling them to make a monthly budget, hire staff, and plan their ministry future.

Typically, when a missionary raises funds, they have a list of regular supporters who contribute at various levels. Let's say that, in order to fulfill their monthly budget, they need twenty people giving $50 a month, ten giving $100 a month, four giving $250 a month, and one giving $1,000 a month. This forms a pyramid shape where the missionary builds his team, and donors know they are part of a team. The solitary guy giving $1,000 a month is an important member of the team. He's the Cyrus for the missionary's support base. The Cyrus is an important team member, but no more important than any other team member. It's easy to say, "I'm doing so much more than anyone else!" Pride sneaks in and can take root before we know it.

Jesus is quick to remind us that, when we give at any level, we are doing nothing more than obeying Him. Whether we give a one-time gift of $10 at God's direction or a monthly contribution of $1,000, we are doing the right thing as long as we are in obedience. As soon as we think we are more important than any other team member, we are no longer giving with a joyful heart—and we are no longer obedient. Just as the widow who dropped two copper coins into the box actually gave more than the rich guys, the $25 team member, in Kingdom terms, can give much more than the Cyrus giver.

Our giving portfolio has grown and, as our passions have changed over the years, a few of the principles listed on the original stewardship philosophy document had to be modified. Our portfolio is full of people. When we look at what we support, it's mostly people who are doing the work that we love. How do we respond when we hear about large projects that are under construction? What do we say when we see schools or hospitals being built? Do we give toward those types of projects as well? Absolutely. As a general rule, people love to give toward something new. They love the idea of growing or expanding a ministry. People love getting new projects off the ground, but rarely do people enjoy giving toward maintenance or administration of the work that is already going on.

Anna and I love the new stuff, too; we get excited when we see a new project. We'll happily help partner with projects like a new building or new program. But, for every new project, it takes twice as much work to keep it going. We love to walk through vacant buildings and dream about how kids could be fed and educated there. As we hear our voices echo off the concrete walls, we can imagine Jesus changing lives in that place. However, we try to keep our focus on the vision, not just the means of getting there. Buildings are great, and they need to be built and bought; however, without the people doing the work, they will once again become vacant.

Therefore, when we help with a project like a building for an organization, we get to know the organization well and commit to keeping it running over the years. This might mean helping find the right people to volunteer or even joining the board.

BIG PROJECTS

When the size of a project is assessed at a larger level of funds—tens of thousands or even millions of dollars—that's not a proposal for a first date. The donor and visionary need to have a well-established relationship for the *ask* to take place. Like an investment in a company, every type of giving investment comes with a certain level of risk.

Loren Cunningham told the story of the beginnings of the organization Youth With a Mission (YWAM) in his excellent book, *Is That Really You, God?* Starting as a group of young people yearning to hear God's voice and sharing the love of Jesus, YWAM grew into an amazing ministry. Operating a fleet of hospital ships is just one of the ministries they started. The ministry's genesis was an incredible journey for everyone involved.

After much prayer and counsel, they obtained their first vessel called the *Maori* in 1973. Its purchase required a down payment of $72,000 (over $400,000 in 2018 dollars), which was provided by a generous English businessman. The Union Steamship Company loaned them the rest, and pledges from specific donors would cover the outstanding balance.

While they began to transform the *Maori* into a hospital, YWAM received some excellent attention from local media. News reporters spoke highly of what they were doing, and the papers loved it. They spoke of the medical care and surgeries that would take place in port cities of needy countries all over the world. One headline read, "Youth Say, 'God Will Give Us The Ship!'" With renovations nearing completion and the final payments coming soon, they announced the ship would be sailing from New Zealand to California in thirty days, the same date the balance of the payment was due. Donations were flowing in, and celebration was in the air!

Suddenly, a few promised donations stopped. A bank in the Philippines declined a major transfer, and the faucet of donations dried up. Not even a trickle. With the deadline for the final payment for the ship only ten days away, Loren spent time in prayer and had a vision:

> I saw myself standing before a crowd of YWAM leaders. I announced with exuberance, "We've got the ship! God has given us the money for the *Maori*!" Then, all of a sudden, I saw a figure standing in the shadows to my left, unnoticed by any of us. I looked closer at His face and saw that He was grieving. Then it hit me—this was Jesus! We were ignoring Him! We were cheering a ship and forgetting Jesus![1]

Loren felt strongly that this could be the end for the ship. He pressed in to hear from God. The leadership team prayed. They went before God as individuals, small groups, large groups, and even held all-night prayer meetings. As a group, they confessed their pride and the turning of their focus away from Jesus. They got an extension on the loan and spent weeks in a long process of waiting and listening. Loren and many YWAM leaders learned profound lessons from God as they waited.

Eventually, the Union Steamship Company closed negotiations, and the ship was lost. When he broke the news to the crew, they were devastated. All their hard work, the promise of so much good to come, had fallen away. Loren was equally concerned about the conversation he would have to have with the man who had made it possible—the $72,000 donor. He made a long-distance phone call and told him the story. He begrudgingly told him about the renovations, the problems with the banks, the vision of Jesus grieving, and the confessions of their sins of idolatry and pride. He explained how the process of humbly seeking Him once again opened the door to hearing God's guidance.

The donor listened intently and then said, "What you're trying to say, Loren, is that you've lost the deposit money."

"That's…that's right."

After a long pause, broken only by the crackle of the cable connection, he spoke, "I consider my money well invested, Loren! God has used it to get your organization humbled before Him. I expect you to move ahead with a special power now. Congratulations!"[2]

Far from a first date, this anonymous English businessman was an incredible encouragement in the midst of what would be classified by any other measure as a colossal failure. Who knows what Jesus had just said to him prior to Loren's call to prepare him for the news?

Loren and his friend shared an understanding of YWAM's long-term mission. They were both more in love with Jesus than the ship and proved it with their finances and efforts. The funding of the *Maori* was much more than a ship; it symbolized an entire group of men and women who knew the importance of drawing near to God. We should remember that giving to a project—a building, ship, or anything substantial—is still investing in people rather than the physical entity. The history the two men shared allowed an expression of brotherly love to be exchanged through a gift of friendship. Eventually, YWAM bought and remodeled a fleet of ships that have sailed to ports all over the world bringing hope and healing.

GIVING FOR NATURAL DISASTERS

Every year, news reports show how hurricanes, tsunamis, tornadoes, and floods devastate various locations around the globe. They show graphic images and release death tolls. These are acts of nature; the people haven't brought this on themselves. People are compassionate and give generously. Knowing this will happen, some organizations have *ready-made fundraisers*: "Call this number and $10 will be charged to your phone bill and will go to the Red Cross for relief effort for Hurricane Harvey."

People are generous. Millions of dollars are donated for each disaster. This type of immediate fundraising is a great picture of people joining with the mission of saving lives! However, this type of quick-response relief is more like a temporary Band-Aid than the long-term reconstruction that needs to take place. Granted, when I watch my son fall off his scooter and scrape his knee, I'm happy to give him a Band-Aid. It helps cover the wound while the healing process takes place, but when he falls down and breaks his leg, he needs more than a Band-Aid. The help that often comes immediately after a disaster is temporary, and once the news coverage dies down the real process of rebuilding starts. Band-Aids are given when what is really needed is long-term reconstruction and care. In addition, sadly, the corruption that accompanies this type of giving is widespread.

Anna and I were already very much involved in Haiti when the 2010 earthquake devastated the country. Scores of organizations sent help in tangible ways—search-and-rescue teams, medical supplies, field hospitals, food, water, temporary housing, and most everything else the country needed. In addition, many millions of dollars were sent as cash donations. While some of it found its destination, millions of dollars never got to the people who were affected. Huge non-governmental organizations (NGOs) responsible for much of the relief efforts received funds that became untraceable. Unfortunately, when thousands—or even millions—of people decide to give, others take advantage of it. A catastrophe is a prime opportunity for corruption.

I mentioned Willem Charles, the founder of Mountain Top Ministries, in Chapter 6 of this book. After this disaster, I asked Willem about his role in the earthquake. He lived through the chaos and saw not only how much was donated to the country but also how little progress was made. He said, "Millions and millions of dollars were given. Most of it never got to the people."

It is common for an organization's bank account to fluctuate widely during a crisis. Enormous needs are everywhere; people have tremendous expenses: food distributions, medical care, rebuilding efforts, and so on. Large donations come in, and the funds increase. Expenses continue, and the funds are dispersed. Meanwhile, communication is chaotic and with wide fluctuation in dollar amounts and the unreliability of accounting practices in some parts of the world, scandalous siphoning of funds to personal pockets occurs. Corruption, inefficiency, and scandals kill fundraising efforts; yet in crisis situations, where the videos of tragedy supersede the stories of corruption, it continues. That's why working with an organization you know, love, and trust is paramount.

STUDENT MISSION TRIPS

What about the students who ask for money to go on a summer mission trip? At the coaching of their team leaders, they often put together an attractive letter, share what they will be doing, and ask for prayer and money. Recently, we got a letter from Samantha, a high-school girl who was going to Mexico on a mission trip. She told us about the upcoming trip, during which they would deliver Bibles and visit an orphanage. She asked us to pray for her during the trip.

She told us her cost for the trip would be $2,400, and she included a little self-addressed card with a box to check indicating the promise of financial support.

When we get communication like this, we almost always help. I can't imagine a better way for young people to learn about God's provision through prayer. When they ask clearly, explaining their vision and plans, God provides the funds they need. I'm happy to give money for these kids as an investment in their knowledge of God's provision. Is there a better way for young people to learn about the character of God as the one who provides, Jehovah-Jireh? Jesus is clear when He talks about giving and prayer: "Keep on asking, and you will receive what you ask for. Keep on seeking, and you will find. Keep on knocking, and the door will be opened to you. For everyone who asks, receives. Everyone who seeks, finds. And to everyone who knocks, the door will be opened" (Matthew 7:7–8).

Most likely, there will be a time in Samantha's life when she needs to depend on God in a major way. Maybe she will be in full-time ministry or even full-time missions, but most likely it will be something less "churchy." Maybe, once she's married with kids, she will be a working mother; both she and her husband could lose their jobs, and they would have no way to care for their family. As she cries out to God for help and provision, with her faith in Him firmly established, she'll know that God will provide—because she would have seen Him provide for her in the past.

We also get similar requests for help with numerous other good causes: the Cancer Research Foundation, Alzheimer's Association, alma maters, and other worthy endeavors. Usually, these requests come in the form of support for a team in a fund-raiser drive or in honor of someone who passed from the named ailment. While this is not our passion, there is absolutely nothing wrong with donating to these causes. In fact, I enjoy giving a certain amount to various causes, but these are not the main thrust of our giving portfolio because they do not align with our giving passions or stewardship philosophy.

THE GIVING CYCLE

The process of evaluating and reviewing our donations is called the Giving Cycle. The planning and strategic aspect of giving is a circular, repeatable exercise that we revisit quarterly or annually. It doesn't happen on its own. We need to set aside time periodically—perhaps with a calendar reminder—to look at our giving mission statement, our giving portfolio, and our giving goals. In our first interaction with a ministry, we research by looking online, talking with the ministry, or even visiting them for a while. When we make the decision to give, we also partner with them in prayer. We are then bound with them at a certain level. After a little time goes by, we re-evaluate; we investigate where our dollars have gone. This is where we ask more questions than we did at first. Is there administrative waste in the organization? Do the dollars really get to the intended ministry? Is progress being made? Do we continue our giving? Increase it? Or move on to another organization? We process the information and maybe give again.

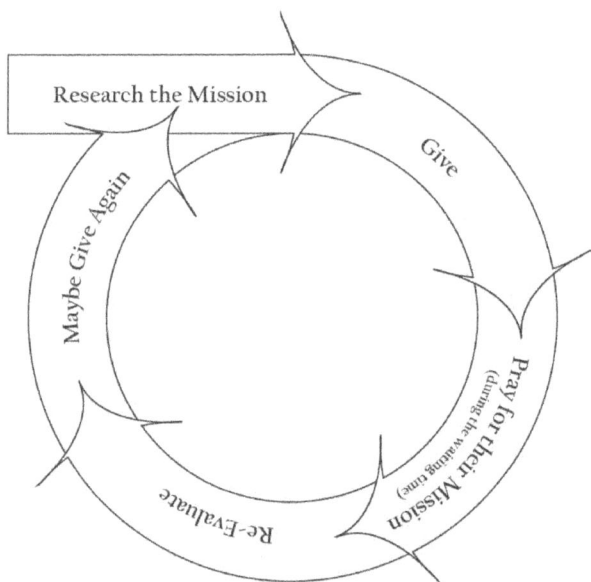

Research the Mission — Give — Pray for their Mission (during the waiting time) — Re-Evaluate — Maybe Give Again

We take time to give in creative new ways, to look back and see what's worked in the past and see what expensive lessons occurred in the giving process. We faithfully evaluate and measure our gifts because we are stewards searching for maximum impact.

But, most importantly, this isn't about *our* goals. Once we start focusing on what *we* want instead of what God wants to do with His money, we lose the reason for our giving. This is all about our amazing God. He has inspired generosity through His Son, Jesus, who was the greatest gift ever given. It's only because of Him that we can give in the first place. It's not about us at all. We need to be sure to spend time in prayer with God over all finances, asking for His wisdom and His leading in our lives when it comes to finances and generosity.

Our giving portfolio has evolved over the years. Anna and I can list our favorite missionaries off the top of our head. We know them well. We can also discuss at length their mission, vision, values, and goals because they line up with our own. Over the years, our giving portfolio has become a part of us. It is much more than a list of people we support; it represents partnerships with people we love. It is a living, breathing part of our lives.

As with anything involving people, though, there are problems. The journey of generosity has its share of unique challenges. We will dive into some of them in the next chapter.

Looking Inside:

1) Based on your passions and giving plan, what does *dating* look like for you? What would it look like to *marry* a ministry or organization with your giving dollars?

2) How can you lead a DTR conversation about a ministry or organization you support?

Taking action:

1) What guidelines could you make concerning giving to individuals?

2) How is a relationship changed when one person gives generously to another?

3) Dave Ramsey says loaning money within families makes Thanksgiving dinner taste different. Have you ever experienced anything like that? Can it be done well, where the relationship grows stronger through generosity?

CHAPTER 12

PITFALLS AND PRAISES

If [your gift] is giving, give generously.

Romans 12:8

Generosity is a great way to show love toward one another, and, when it is exercised well, everybody rejoices. However, as sinful people, we have a weak underbelly. Sins such as pride and greed can wreak havoc in our lives and disrupt everything, including generosity. I've been blessed to witness firsthand some amazing giving stories. I've also had a front-row seat to some giving disasters. As we broaden our view of a life of giving, let's take a look at some of the ways giving goes right—*and wrong*.

ANANIAS AND SAPPHIRA: GIVING GONE WRONG

We get to see the church being born in the first part of the book of Acts. The people began to share with one another in selfless ways as an outpouring of their faith in Jesus Christ. People gave generously as the church grew, and the young church began to find its legs. Many of the believers had seen and heard Jesus in person, had been at the Sermon on the Mount, and had heard Him teach. Now they were discovering who He really was! Their growth in faith was evident in their generosity.

The early believers' treatment of money revealed their generous hearts. For a variety of reasons, it had become normal for people to sell their land and give the proceeds to the nascent church. Can you imagine that? It became normal for a man to come home from work after a long hard day and greet his wife saying, "You know, honey, let's sell the pasture on the north end and give the money to Peter."

She'd smile and say, "Yep, the Johnsons had that unexpected medical expense. Maybe Peter will give it to them. Sounds good to me." They would sell the property and deliver a pouch of silver coins to the apostles for disbursement as they saw fit. Giving investments to the church for them to distribute to the needy became a common practice!

The fifth chapter of Acts introduces us to a couple having this kind of conversation. A man named Ananias came home after work one day and greeted his wife, "Sapphira, don't you think we could sell the field over by the Akerman's olive orchard?"

Sapphira said, "Sure, dear. Do you want to give the money away like a lot of people are doing, or are we going to get that new camel we've been talking about?"

Ananias stroked his bearded chin, "It's a pretty big field. I think we can do both!"

They sold the property, kept back for themselves a small stack of silver coins, and laid the rest at the apostles' feet. Ananias gave the public appearance of being generous, but he lied about his giving.

Peter was not gentle. "Ananias, why have you let Satan fill your heart? You lied to the Holy Spirit, and you kept some of the money for yourself. The property was yours to sell or not sell, as you wished. And after selling it, the money was also yours to give away. How could you do a thing like this? You weren't lying to us but to God!" (Acts 5:3–5).

God struck him dead on the spot.

You would think this would be the end of the story. Not at all! About three hours later, Sapphira dismounted her brand-new camel and came sauntering into the temple looking for her husband. Peter quizzed her, "Was this the price you and your husband received for your land?" (Acts 6:8). She lied and said yes. Immediately, she also fell down and died.

Imagine the backlash the church must have gone through after this happened. The Twitter storm must have been incredible. Facebook and Instagram accounts were going crazy. People were talking about this more than anything they had ever seen.

Why did God strike them dead for such a seemingly small indiscretion? It was just a little lie! Didn't they just slip a tiny fib in there? After all, they gave generously. They didn't have to give at all, and they gave a tremendous amount directly to Peter. How can this be seen as being repulsive or wrong? Why did it happen?

It bears repeating: money reveals the heart. Every penny that passes through our hands tells a little bit more about our relationship with God. When Ananias and Sapphira lied about the money, they lied to the Holy Spirit about a lot of things. They lied about how much they received for the sale of the land. They lied about holding some back for themselves. They lied by implying their hearts were generous because they gave everything they had. It seemed small to them. Plus, they needed a new camel, and this was God's timely way of providing that perfect, one-humped transportation they needed for their business. What it revealed was so much more than that.

God didn't tolerate it.

Money is important to God because money reveals the heart. You could say this story really isn't about money at all. It's about the condition of the heart. The silver that passed through Ananias and Sapphira's hands showed who they were deep inside. They wanted to look generous, but they also prioritized their own wants above their integrity.

God wants us to understand who He is. He wants us to know how much He loves us, and when we are blessed, He wants us to share generously. In doing so, we will take hold of that which is truly life, but if we lie about our generosity, holding back for ourselves something we say we are giving away, we are in danger of the wrath of an all-powerful God.

The lesson from Ananias and Sapphira is real and serious. It's not saying, "God's gonna get you if you try to deceive Him." Rather, it seems to be an isolated case of judgment at a time when the Holy Spirit was moving in great ways and was directly opposed by people who had their own agenda. God saw through their deception and judged swiftly. One wonders if the two of them ever had a true relationship with Jesus in the first place.

This is the only New Testament story of its kind, yet the Old Testament has a few like it—including the account of Achan's sin. In Joshua 6 and 7, we read that Israel was taking the Promised Land. After they marched around Jericho, the walls fell in dramatic fashion. Joshua ordered the men not to take any plunder for themselves as they stormed the city. While rummaging through Jericho's homes, a soldier named Achan found a beautiful robe, as well as some silver and gold. He secretly brought them back to the camp and hid them in his tent. Israel was routed in their very next battle, and eventually Achan's sin was discovered. That day, he and his entire household were stoned to death. The event taught the nation of Israel that God wasn't joking with the rules regarding His rules.

When God's presence and power are openly manifest, He requires a higher level of holiness from us. In each of these instances, God was doing important things that reached far beyond the punishment of a single individual. Ananias and Sapphira's story represents a lesson on the sovereignty of God and who we are in relation to Him. I don't think we need to live in fear of being struck dead if we sin, but we need to know the power and sovereignty of the amazing God we serve. We need to be honest and up front with Him and His representatives when we give. Giving is an extension of our relationship with God in which we do what He asks; it's not an opportunity for us to try to look good in front of others.

I want to point out one more thing before we leave this story. When Peter scolded Ananias, he didn't say, "You should have given all the money!" Rather, he said, "The property was yours to sell or not sell, as you wished. And after selling it, the money was also yours to give away" (Acts 5:4)."

This is an important point: the property was his. The church didn't own it; the apostles didn't ask him to sell it, nor did they tell him to give the money away. After he sold it, the money was his. The problem Ananias had wasn't that he didn't give enough; in fact, he was very generous. The problem was that his heart wasn't right before God; he wanted to look good before the community. He lied.

It is true that God owns everything, and when we say we have property that we own, sell, or give away, that is also true. God has provided property for us to manage as best we can with Him in mind.

GREAT GOALS FOR GIVING

Just about everyone makes goals at some point in their life. In sports, weight loss, Bible study, schoolwork, and at our vocations, our activities are best fulfilled by the pursuit of tangible achievements. They provide inspiration and motivation to challenge us to higher levels of performance. Giving goals can be just as powerful as long as they are set with the proper focus. Imagine the joy of planning to give away a large amount of money this year and accomplishing your goal. (The number can be anything you feel God telling you). Perhaps you have a lifetime number you would love to achieve.

Francis Chan, author of *Crazy Love* and former teaching pastor of Cornerstone Community Church in Simi Valley, California, told the wonderful story of praying about his personal finances when it struck him that he should ask God how much to give. So he did. At the beginning of January, he asked, "Over the next twelve months, how much should I give?"

He waited, then got a number: $30,000.

He thought, *Are you kidding me? That's the amount I made last year.*

Chan was experienced in knowing God's voice, so he humbly committed to the challenge. He was intentional with his giving the next year. As more came in, he just gave and gave. By the end of the year, he looked back and saw that he had met his goal. Once again, he approached God with the question, "How much do you want us to give next year?"

God replied, "$50,000."

Now, that was a stretch! If the previous year had been a ridiculous goal, how could $50,000 possibly happen? He accepted it on faith and gave. As more money came in here and there from one source or another, Chan continued to give. By the end of the year, he was amazed by God's provision, and he had met his giving goal.

This was incredible! A man who made $30,000 per year was, within two years, giving away almost twice that amount! The story doesn't stop there. He asked God the same question the following January. This time the answer came back, "$100,000."

At this point, he was like the character in *Brewster's Millions*, the 1985 movie starring Richard Pryor. Chan didn't want the money. He didn't want a new house, better cars, or a better standard of living. He had his budget, his finish line, and a giving account, and he was not surprised at all when the giving goal was accomplished by that December.

Then, when January rolled around and he asked again, God said, "One million dollars!"

Chan was simply overwhelmed. *How?*, he thought. *That doesn't even make sense!*

He remained faithful to the plan. God kept shoveling money in, and every time more came in, he just shoveled it out again. God had a bigger shovel.

God kept shoveling money in, and every time more came in, he just shoveled it out again. God had a bigger shovel.

I hope every single person who reads this book will have a story like Francis Chan's. All of us can hear from God, and if He wants to set out a giving goal for us, He can do amazing things in our hearts through the process.

Competitive Giving

While giving goals can lead to some incredible tales of generosity, we can get sidetracked in giving if we use it as a competition. I'm a pretty competitive guy, and I know if I set a goal, I'll work extra hard to accomplish it. I've used goals in athletics, scholastic achievements, and even at the office. On the other hand, goal-driven accomplishments in giving can be an unhealthy redirection of focus.

Seamus and Rommel had been friends for five years. They worked the night shift together at a Hormel plant packing Spam. Seamus was known for his vivacious charisma and ability to tell stories that drew crowds wherever he went, and, with his amiable personality, he was a natural leader. Moreover, there was never a conversation he didn't have an opinion on or a subject on which he wouldn't offer advice. Rommel, on the other hand, was mild mannered and avoided controversy. They enjoyed one another's company and were inseparable.

The two of them were also pathologically competitive. They found ways to turn any routine activity into a competition. Both were also dedicated Christ followers and volunteered in a number of ways inside and outside of their church. Rommel, who was growing in his dedication to generous living, had set his finish line and was excited about the giving opportunities he was finding. He told Seamus about his new adventure, and, although Seamus listened intently, it was clear that he wouldn't join Rommel in the journey.

On one of their weekend dinners together, Rommel and Seamus were alone debating sports franchises around a bowl of chips and guacamole. Rommel changed the subject and shared about his giving experiences while Seamus stayed quiet. After a few stories, Rommel said, "I'm throwing down the gauntlet. I've got a challenge for you."

Instantly, Seamus's competitive nature was engaged. His eyes widened, and he joked, "A bit uncharacteristic of you. I'm all ears."

"Over the next twelve months, I challenge you to a giving competition. Just you against me, giving to Christian organizations. Let's see who donates the most!"

Seamus smirked and tilted his head off to the side, but he remained silent. Surprised by the absence of a typical verbose comeback, Rommel continued, "We both make about the same amount, so let's make it a challenge. You get to set the parameters. You can make it total dollars given. You can make it a percentage of your income. Make the game whatever you want. I still think I'll beat you. Let's see who gives more!"

Seamus was silent. He dipped his chip in the guacamole and tossed it in his mouth. Rommel could sense a bit of tension in the room, and before long, he changed the subject. They never mentioned the challenge again.

I can imagine Jesus enjoying guacamole with them at the party. He wasn't invited into this conversation at all. Had He been a part of it, He would have laughed with the two of them as the contest was suggested, and maybe He would have instructed them both in the nature of biblical stewardship. I can imagine Him saying, "It's not about proving that you are better than anyone else. If you make a competition out of giving, then the focus is on you, not me. In order for you to use resources the way I want you to, it has to be about me—never about beating the other guy."

Patty's Challenge

My mother told me the story of her good friend Patty, a divorcée raising her four kids, working as a part-time real estate agent. She sold houses when she was able and picked up odd jobs on the side to make ends meet. In 1972, Patty's church was building a new facility, and they were in the middle of the capital campaign. Standing at the entrance to the church, the pastor shook hands with each parishioner as they exited. Patty reached out to say good-bye, and the pastor stopped her and said, "Patty, I've got something that I really need to tell you, but I'm not sure how. Maybe we could meet in my office later on."

"Oh, Pastor," she said. "Just tell me and get it over with." Patty was known to get right to the point.

He looked around and knew that they were holding up the line, so he decided to just deliver his message. "I've been praying about this capital campaign. It's pretty overwhelming for me. As I've been talking with God, the Lord has made it clear to me that you are to give a million dollars to our building fund."

Patty let out a guffaw that turned heads all around them.

"I'm just delivering the message," the pastor said sheepishly.

"Whatever," she blurted out as she reached down to gather her kids and make her exit.

The pastor held his hands out defensively and said, "Just think about starting by pledging $1,000 per month."

Patty treated his final comment as if it were an insult to dodge. She piled her kids into their station wagon and headed home. On the way home, all she could think about were his words. She laughed like Sarah did when Abraham was given the message that they would have a son, but all the while, the message began to take root. It was all she could think about, because she knew it was from God. She was also inspired to go ahead and pledge $1,000 a month. She was dedicated to living for Jesus, and a huge part of that is obeying Jesus when He asks us to do something. The last thing she wanted was to be disobedient to God Almighty! She filled out a pledge card the following Sunday. She committed to giving $1,000 a month—with no ability to do so. For Patty, it was a leap of faith.

Within the next few weeks, her houses started selling quicker than they ever had. More and more homes were listed and sold. She gained a reputation as an excellent real estate agent, and people referred their friends and family to her. Soon she was selling more in a week than she used to sell in a month, and she no longer had to pick up extra work outside real estate.

Week after week, houses sold. She expanded into commercial property, then rentals, and then even more. All the while, her giving increased until it went well beyond her $1,000 a month pledge. As years passed by, the Lord continued to bless Patty's business, and she continued to increase her giving. Generosity became a normal part of her daily routine. Before she passed away, Patty looked back on her lifelong history of generosity and mentally added up her giving. She found that she had far exceeded the $1 million pledge for the building fund that had started it all. She simply followed God's inspiration to be generous, and, as she was able, she gave more and more. Through her benevolence, thousands of people have been blessed.

Gary's First Paycheck

Gary had always been faithful in tithing. Giving ten percent was a normal part of his routine since childhood, even as a college student, with an unending mountain of college debt. With his graduation date coming, he was looking forward to beginning his first "adult" job and greatly anticipated a real paycheck. He would earn over $2,500 in a single month! He had never seen so much money flow his direction without having to promise to pay it back.

Gary's wonderful young church had just embarked on a three-year fundraising campaign to raise several hundred thousand dollars for a new facility. The church was filled with every type of individual: college students to professors and janitors to business presidents. A less homogenous mixture would be hard to create. Some had great jobs and had accumulated wealth, while others, including Gary, were overburdened with student-loan debt. There was seemingly no good way to ask for money from such a motley crew until the church announced the slogan "Not equal giving, but equal sacrifice." This is a fantastic campaign slogan that has been used in churches all across the world.

Repeated over and over again, "Not equal giving, but equal sacrifice" became their mantra. It was clear that they could not all give equally, yet it was also becoming clear that they all could sacrifice financially to advance the kingdom of God. One of the elders in the church, a man of God who made his living as a janitor, was not making a tremendous amount, but he was dedicated to the campaign. He looked over his monthly expenses and saw that he had a candy bar and a soda every day at work. If he cut out those snacks, he could give $2 a day, which worked out to $500 each year. He realized that sacrificing a soda and candy bar wasn't really that much of a sacrifice, so he imagined other ways to save and ultimately pledged $1,000 a year toward the campaign.

Gary sat in the folding chairs of the new church listening as others shared their stories and made pledges. He wanted to do his part. When God graciously softened his heart, suddenly giving didn't seem like a big sacrifice to him. He had never received a real wage, so it wasn't much of a sacrifice for him to give. He asked God how much he should pledge and quickly got the answer that he should give the amount of his first paycheck. He

> *He gave away his entire first paycheck, the firstfruits of his career.*

made his pledge, and, when the check came a few weeks later, he gave that amount and kept living frugally as he had been. The following month, he started using his paycheck to cover bills and start repaying loans.

Most people would say that Gary was sacrificing tremendously since he gave away his entire first paycheck, the firstfruits of his career. He didn't feel that way at all. He just obeyed and gave what God had provided.

THE PULSE OF THE BODY

This is how the church body works. As stewards, we have the privilege of interacting with our heavenly Father and ministering to the needs of His children throughout the world. Without the Holy Spirit prompting our giving, the whole process could become cold and calculated. Divine promptings are the pulse in the church body, and giving allows the gospel work to move forward.

A common theme weaves through the fabric of each of these stories. Giving, when done as an outpouring from a relationship with Jesus Christ, reveals our hearts as they grow to be like His. Sometimes God is doing far more than we can see, and when we're faced with a giving opportunity, He may actually want us to say no so that other people can be involved and draw near to Him in the process. We'll explore that in the next chapter.

Looking inside:

1) Ananias and Sapphira were generous but tried to look better than they really were.

    a. Recall and describe a time when you tried to look better than you really were.

    b. Describe a time when you claimed to be more generous than you actually were.

2) In what ways are giving goals helpful?

3) How can they be harmful?

Taking action:

1) Ask God what kind of giving goal He wants you to strive for. Be ready to commit to whatever He tells you, no matter how crazy or unrealistic it seems.

CHAPTER 13

JOY IN SAYING NO

He did all this so you would never say to yourself, "I have achieved this wealth with my own strength and energy." Remember the Lord your God. He is the one who gives you power to be successful.

Deuteronomy 8:17–18

I love saying yes.
I love hearing the word yes.
When people ask if I have a story about my kids, the answer is always *yes*! When Anna and I got married, we both got to say, "I do." Anytime our schedule allows, when I ask Anna if she wants to go out on a date, I love it when she says, "You betcha!"

In our giving portfolio, we've had many opportunities to affirm our connection with a ministry's mission by joining them with a giant yes. There are plenty of times that God also works through a big fat no.

When faced with an opportunity to give, we refer to our stewardship philosophy as our guiding document. Inevitably, this means there are multitudes of legitimate, God-inspired, holy ministries that we will not support. This leads to discomfort when someone makes a request for aid that does not fall within the boundaries of our plan.

THE MINIVAN

Brian Pendleton (whom I mentioned in Chapter 8) has been faithful with his calling to ministry at IHOPKC for years, and we've come to love him as a brother. He sent me a well-written, printed form letter saying their family would soon be buying a minivan and requested our help. Brian's only vehicle was a fourteen-year-old Saturn with over 215,000 miles on it and no air conditioning. Their other car, a Jeep, had been rear-ended and was totaled, and they needed a quality vehicle. They had their eye on a silver, three-year-old Chrysler Town and Country minivan with 22,000 miles and were hoping that God would allow them to buy it.

Honestly, I didn't give much thought to the letter. It wasn't something I was excited about; I didn't think about giving—or *not* giving—toward it. A week later, Brian sent me a text asking if I could talk about something. He was being strategic, and I recognized what he was doing. I was also strategic; before I talked with Brian, I asked Jesus, *Should I give extra to Brian to help with the minivan?*

Jesus was pretty clear with a gentle nudge that reminded me of our stewardship philosophy. I mentally reviewed the document. I also thought about our friendship with Brian and our support over the years. From what I had read in our philosophy, it was clear that we were to support him but not help out with this project. The answer was clear: "Stick to the philosophy."

Shortly after the text message, I received a call from Brian. I was happy to hear his voice, but I dreaded the inevitable conversation. Brian is an accomplished extrovert and rarely has short conversations. In fact, most of his calls are at least forty-five minutes because he loves people and genuinely wants to engage in their lives. After small talk and discussing how each of our children were doing, he said, "So, we are in the process of raising money to buy a good-quality, used minivan for our family."

I smiled as he described the vehicle and proceeded to let me know the specifics. I knew he was being responsible in caring for his family, but I also knew my heart was not in the minivan—not at all.

I interrupted, "I think that's a great idea. Anna and I have a pretty clear stewardship philosophy for what we give toward and what we don't, and this is really not part of our philosophy." I began to feel a bit sheepish but continued, "So, I'm sorry, but I'm going to have to say no."

Brian replied, "That's fantastic! It's wonderful that you know where your passions lie and have the discipline to give where God directs."

I was shocked at his response. While I didn't expect him to whine and complain about my rejection, I also didn't expect a parade for following God's call in our lives. Brian wasn't done. He continued, "That just gave me so much joy. I'm so happy for you two. Great! Hey, have I told you about the progress we've made in the ministry?" He immediately shifted gears; we discussed his work, and I thoroughly enjoyed the rest of the conversation.

I couldn't help but laugh. His smile was evident through the cell phone connection. Brian's friendship and our support were independent of one another. I realized that if I stopped supporting him or had never supported him at all he would still be the same great friend. The remainder of the call was lighthearted. Then he was on to his next calls.

A year later, Brian and I discussed the minivan project. Brian recalled, "Fundraising is a funny thing. I love it because it's really about relationships. I love talking with my friends, but I absolutely hate making the phone calls. When we needed the minivan, I worked hard on the initial letter and sent it out to my core ministry partners. I knew I had twenty-two people I needed to call. I dreaded it. I decided to call my friend Andy first for a few reasons." I loved that he was talking about me in the third person. "First, he's a real friend. We've talked about finances a number of times over the years, so it wouldn't be awkward talking about money with him. Secondly, he will probably say yes, which will get my ball rolling right from the start."

I laughed thinking that I had done quite the opposite of getting the fundraising started for him. Brian continued, "When you said no, you didn't just say, 'Nah, I don't feel like it.' You explained that you were keeping to your stewardship philosophy. That's what filled my heart with joy. You said no with a specific purpose in mind."

This conversation could have had a floundering feel to it, but Brian was incredibly gracious. He explained, "Most people don't have a giving plan. I sure don't. But you do. I'm a servant of the same God you are, so the last thing I would want is for you to steward your money poorly or for me to extract money from you somehow."

I chuckled at the thought of him forcing me to give in a way that didn't line up with what God desired. He continued, "It may sound crazy, but at that moment, hearing about your giving plan empowered me. I was encouraged to reach out to the other twenty-one people and make those dreaded phone calls."

"So, you ended up getting the minivan, right?"

"Yes, the process was pretty involved. Of the calls I made, four people said no, including you." Once again he laughed out loud. "The donations ranged from $150, all the way up to $1,000. We had four of those." I wonder what types of lessons God taught people through each of the donations.

"And the minivan is working out well for you?" I asked.

"Absolutely, it's been a huge blessing to our family." He paused for a minute, then continued, "You know, come to think of it, I don't know what your passions for giving are. That's a good thing. It means that there is no way for me to manipulate your giving."

Brian talked a little bit more and stumbled onto the subject of his education in fundraising. "The guy who teaches fundraising at IHOPKC is like you. He knows what his passions are and what they aren't. On occasion, he will say no and doesn't mind saying no without risk of disapproval. Fundraising is the process of developing a relationship. When I ask someone to join us in the IHOPKC mission, it's merely to see if it's a partnership we want to have together. He can say no, and so can I. It's a two-way street; even if he says yes and offers to give, I can still say, 'No, thanks.' We are just seeing if this is a good fit."

He concluded, "When we are relieved of the anxiety about being rejected or feeling humiliated, asking is easier. When we no longer risk depression when someone says, 'No, I'm not going to get involved in your ministry,' then fundraising brings joy. When we have gained the freedom to ask without fear, to love fundraising as a form of ministry, then fundraising is a healthy part of our spiritual lives."

Again, we laughed at God's providential grace in the development of our healthy, brotherly relationship.

SAYING NO SO OTHERS CAN SAY YES

Anna and I have been thrilled to be a part of the Dubuque Dream Center since its inception. The director, Robert Kimble, had a vision for working with the underprivileged youth in our downtown area. As an educator and coach, he has worked with kids for decades and has a track record of connecting with students and athletes in a way that leads to them having a profound impact in their lives. We had been with him while he developed the Dream Center's focus on at-risk kids with their academic center. He wanted to bridge the gap between schools, students, and parents. The Dream Center provides structured after-school programs and activities where youth can build relationships with caring adults, have a safe place to belong, and participate in value-driven programs and activities.

Anna and I routinely had dinner with Robert and his wife, Nelli, every few months. At one of our meals, I was getting ready to make my "What do you need?" pitch, but before I could get the question out, the visionary leader launched into his six-part plan for the next year. They needed additional volunteers and staff, transportation, gym renovation, and academic center technology. I asked about the tech needs, and he explained that the computers the students used were old hand-me-downs from the city and weren't working well for the kids.

He said, "We need forty iPads. That's what they use at the premier schools, and the teachers said that they would improve the tutoring sessions immensely." The rest of the dinner was relaxed and fun, and we all enjoyed our time together.

We parted with hope; while we had no specific plans on how to help, I was grateful for the clarity of his discussion. He listed six things, but only one thing resonated with me: the Dream Center needed iPads, and I dreamt about how the technology would help the kids. I considered issues such as theft and damage of the fragile tablets and knew Robert had a good track record of handling such issues with diligence and discipline. The current computers were locked up in a closet. When they were checked out, they were used under supervision and then returned. There was no problem with the administration of the project. They just needed the iPads.

I looked up iPads online, found out what models the schools used, and then dropped in at the local electronics store to talk with the manager about helping with a donation. The store manager didn't offer to donate forty iPads, but he referred me up the ladder to his boss. I was unable to connect with that person after several attempts.

For the next few days, iPads were constantly on my mind. I knew the impact they would have and wanted to find a way to get it done. Anna and I talked about it, and we weren't sure how we were supposed to be involved. We asked God how we could help with this, but we got no answer. He didn't even give me a nudge or hint of anything at all. I was sold on the idea, but we weren't getting a green light to do this ourselves. I definitely had the passion for the project, but in terms of funding it, God seemed to be saying no.

Not long afterward, I was at a meeting with some church leaders. When the meeting adjourned and we were literally out the door, I remembered the iPads. I stopped everybody and tossed out an idea. "Hey! Do any of you think we could help with a fundraiser for iPads for the Dream Center?" Fortunately, everybody there was quite familiar with the Dream Center and had helped before in various capacities.

I explained the need for forty iPads and was about to run some numbers to see what kind of funds we would be talking about when my friend Brian Schatz stepped forward. As the COO of a large medical group, he stated, "My company has a bunch of those that we had to buy but aren't using." They had just upgraded their computer system and ended up with a surplus of iPads. His brow furrowed as he pondered the process. "It will take a vote from the board. I'll check it out and see what we can do."

Brian contacted the information technology department and inquired about the iPads. He also spoke with the accounting department about how to handle the asset and spent some time with his boss and peers drumming up support for the project. Within a few weeks, he invited Robert to a Medical Associates board meeting to share his vision.

Robert simply talked about his vision to mobilize youth and families to build on Dr. Martin Luther King's dream of transforming communities by embracing, empowering, and unifying those who live there. He told a few stories about kids in the program and showed how the staff strives to inspire vision and purpose through strengthening families and building community.

Robert concluded by talking about the existing computers in the academic center, and he clearly told the doctors how iPads would help the kids meet their scholastic goals as the volunteer teachers instilled the value of education and tracked the progress of each child individually. After Robert departed, Brian opened the conversation to further discussion. The doctors were encouraged and happy to help, and they voted to give the iPads. It didn't take long for the IT department to tweak the programming, and soon the iPads were in the hands of aspiring students at the Dream Center.

Not only did God orchestrate a tremendous gift, but He also worked significantly in Brian Schatz's heart. He had been struggling with seeing God directly at work in his job and had asked God for clarification. God showed up clearly and re-established His sovereignty over the business.

Looking at the process from an arm's length, I had no idea why I wasn't given the green light to help financially with the iPads. Looking back, however, I can see how God united dozens of people around a central vision bound by generosity. God did a lot in the hearts of many people as He broke through the barrier of social status and provided a way for a large number of men and women to join in the vision of the Dream Center.

There are many ways of saying no to a gift, project, or program. When we have our stewardship philosophy clear and understood, it becomes easier to say no. God sometimes tells us to say no so He can provide a creative way for others to break through and say yes. My role in this project was not to be a donor, but to act as a connector, so other people could be a part of God's plan.

Looking inside:

1) God didn't give Anna and me the green light to pay for the iPads because He wanted to bless others through the opportunity to give. What does that tell us about God's plans for His resources? What was God doing in Brian Schatz's heart through the iPads?

2) As you target your giving according to your plan, how will you know when to say no?

3) How does saying yes out of guilt or lack of direction for our giving hinder God's plan for the use of His resources?

Taking action:

1) In what type of situations is it appropriate to decline a request for funds?

2) What are some ways you could tactfully turn down a request for help if you knew it wasn't what God wanted you to do?

CHAPTER 14

RAISE YOUR HAND

He was a devout, God-fearing man, as was everyone in his household. He gave generously to the poor and prayed regularly to God.

Acts 10:2

"At the Dream Center, we currently serve ninety kids every day. We give each one of them a community to belong in, a structure, and a hope for a future. Many of them are no longer C and D students, but they are getting A's and B's." With a microphone in hand, the speaker walked through a crowd of formally dressed men and women in a beautiful ballroom. At-risk youth were tutored, and they were given opportunities through structured sports they otherwise would not have had. The Dream Center wanted to expand to serve upwards of two hundred kids in their facility, and they needed money to make it happen.

The speaker challenged the potential donors seated at dinner tables, "Who will give to support the kids? It costs $1,200 per child each year. Who will join me in supporting the kids? Let's start with four kids! Who will support four kids? Just for fun, we'll round the number up, who can give $5,000?"

Across the room, several people raised their hands. As a board member, I was pleased. I had been with the Dream Center from its inception and had supported them in a variety of ways, but never

151

publicly. I had hoped for a good showing and was happy to see hands raised, but I was uncomfortable. Never before had I lifted my hand in this kind of situation. I sat in my seat recalling Jesus' warning in Matthew 6:1, "Watch out! Don't do your good deeds publicly, to be admired by others, for you will lose the reward from your Father in heaven." I didn't want to raise my hand, yet I saw one board member after another with hands in the air.

The program was concluding. They had already given the speeches, sung the songs, and told the stories that night. It was well into the time to make the *ask*, and the challenge was clear. "Raise your hand if you want to join us in supporting the children."

I was the only board member left, yet my hands remained in my lap. I had already filled out the commitment card, and I knew what I was going to give. In my mind, that was all that was necessary, and it was better than making a public declaration.

But was it? Should I have raised my hand? Would one additional hand in the air have helped anything? Would my hand help build the momentum that the Dream Center needed? If enough hands went up, would we have built a critical mass that started a movement to bring in a flood of funding?

A few moments passed, then the challenge shifted. The speaker went in another direction; I had missed my chance. I had made my choice.

Would it have been better for me to raise my hand?

TOMS SHOES

Let's look at another example where the same issue comes up in a much different fashion. I love Toms Shoes. Blake Mycoskie, an entrepreneur from Arlington, Texas, founded Toms in 2006 to design and sell shoes and eyewear. From its beginning, Toms was committed to philanthropy. For each pair of shoes they sell, Toms donates a new pair of shoes to an impoverished child. Likewise, when they sell a pair of sunglasses, part of the profit is used to save or restore the eyesight of people in developing countries. In addition, they also provide clean water supplies and are involved in other worthy projects.

Giving has always been a part of the Toms company's DNA. Through social media and their website, it is easy to see their giving. They are giving out loud, and people love it. The company has grown quickly, from a startup to a $600 million valuation in just over a decade. Their shoes and sunglasses are high quality with trendy styles, but their success is not only due to their excellent products; some people actually prefer Toms products simply because they know their money is going to help people in developing nations.

The company has grown and faced all the challenges of a typical organization. At the same time, however, their giving has grown, and they have faced equally challenging elements of partnering with non-governmental organizations (NGOs) across the globe.

Jesus says to do your giving privately, to not sound the trumpet and let everybody know what you are doing. The website and social media are modern-day trumpets, and Toms is definitely getting their message out. How can what they are doing be considered bad? They are doing so much good for so many people. How can we say that it is wrong?

Toms is not alone. For centuries, businesses have earmarked portions of their revenue for charitable causes. Thousands of businesses give generously every year. While the primary reason for charitable giving may be to benefit the people and groups involved, it also makes employees feel good when their employers are generous. This, in turn, helps the company.

Whether it's through direct employee giving—in the form of volunteering or charitable donations—or the company itself sponsoring a cause, employees who frequently participate in volunteer activities in the workplace are twice as likely to report being "very satisfied" with their careers. Employee engagement through a cause is a vital means by which to strengthen employee relationships, enhance employee morale, and even build critical skill sets and expertise.[1] The benefits of corporate generosity are clear, especially when businesses honor their employees' wishes.

WHY WE GIVE

Christians give for all kinds of reasons. When Jesus takes His throne in your life, things change. His ways are higher than our ways, and His thoughts are higher than our thoughts (Isaiah 55:9). As we seek Him and draw near to Him, our lives tend to reflect His character. Our lives begin to show more and more love, joy, peace, patience, kindness, goodness, faithfulness, gentleness, and self-control (Galatians 5:22). People give generously out of love and kindness. Some give out of compassion. Others may give for other Christian purposes: because they love Him, serve Him, and obey Him. Perhaps they do it in faith that their gift will further the kingdom of God.

When it comes to giving, there is also the concept of being rewarded. Let's review what Jesus said again. When He was talking about generosity, He didn't say that giving in front of others was bad. He didn't say we should never let *anyone* know what we are doing. Instead, He said that, if you do your giving out loud, then you have already received your reward in full (Matthew 6:2).

He also says that, with this kind of giving, you will have no reward from your Father in heaven (Matthew 6:1). What reward is He talking about? As we've discussed in previous chapters, God has a heavenly bank account in each of our names. When an act of sacrificial giving is done, then a corresponding deposit is made in the heavenly account. Jesus is specific in saying that we are to lay up treasures for ourselves in heaven (Matthew 6:20). When we give without drawing attention to ourselves, God makes a deposit into our heavenly bank account. This is not based on the dollar amount but rather on the heart behind the gift (Mark 12:42 and Luke 21:2).

Does that mean I shouldn't raise my hand at a fundraiser? Does it mean I shouldn't buy Toms shoes? How can we reconcile these two diametrically opposed issues?

Are corporate businesses that give to charity wrong? I don't think so. Toms is a great business! What they are doing with the profits is fantastic; they can have an incredible impact for good with the vast collection of giving they are able to do. When Toms practices giving, they are receiving their reward in full. This reward comes in terms of satisfied employees, growth of their business, and a reputation for philanthropy. Toms should be celebrated as a business that is doing amazing things. The only downside in the way Toms is operating is that there is no further reward on the other side of heaven. They have received their reward in full, and that's appropriate. The giving has its purpose, which is to build their business. They haven't done anything wrong and are receiving their reward.

SHOULD I RAISE MY HAND?

The highest form of generosity is when it is done anonymously, but there are times when it is helpful to build momentum in a fundraising event and raise your hand. There are times when corporate generosity allows large numbers of people to join in an effort.

It's proper to give aloud, but when you do so, you have just received your reward in full. If I raise my hand, I want to be raising it for the right reasons, with an appropriate attitude in my heart. I do not desire to be seen as a giver and build my reputation; rather, I want to build the mission. I may help build momentum and allow many others to join alongside the mission, and in the process, I may have just received my reward.

So, yes, since that day at the Dream Center fundraiser, I've changed my mind about public giving, and I have decided to occasionally raise my hand to help the mission build momentum. But that's not my only type of giving.

I set aside a certain percentage of my giving for giving aloud. A small amount of our giving each year is used in this way. When I raise my hand for supporting children, I'll be happy to do so. I'm privileged to help build support for the mission. The remaining percentage of our giving is done in a manner where the right hand does not know what the left hand is doing, so my Father who sees what is done in secret will bless me with a heavenly reward (Matthew 6:3).

There are a few ways that raising your hand is helpful—and countless ways it is not. For instance, by listening to folks share their testimonies at Generous Giving conferences, I felt they had just raised their hand and helped me understand what God was up to in their lives. This inspired me to continue with our stewardship philosophy from my Goose Island experience. Likewise, I don't mind raising my hand by sharing my Goose Island story. My hope is that sharing what God has done in my life will inspire people all over the world to enjoy the journey of generosity. This includes the rewards on the other side of heaven.

If a prayer warrior never tells anyone that she is down on her knees in prayer for an hour every day, then how could anybody follow her example? Certainly, it isn't proper for her to go out on a street corner and brag about how holy she is and how she prays continuously, but sharing her passion for Jesus and her discipline in prayer can be enormously helpful when done in the proper setting. We all learn from one another's stories. That said, there are limits to what kind of hand-raising I'll participate in. I don't expect you to ever see my name on the side of a building. While I have no problem with folks who name buildings or entire colleges after themselves or posthumously honor a loved one, it is not something that is in our stewardship philosophy. The vast majority of our giving will be behind the scenes, following our passions and God's direction.

I don't pretend to have it all figured out, but as I read through Matthew 6 and listen to the heart of God in relation to giving, I think it is permissible and helpful to raise your hand in certain circumstances and occasionally give out loud. That's at least how I interpret the Scripture.

Looking inside:

1) Dictionary.com defines *philanthropy* as:

> An altruistic concern for human welfare and advancement, usually manifested by donations of money, property, or work to needy persons, or institutions of learning or hospitals, and by generosity to other socially useful purposes.[2]

Is there a difference between *philanthropy* and *biblical stewardship*?

2) Think about times in your giving when you've told people what you've done. Was it helpful to tell the stories or not?

 a. Who was glorified by telling the story?

 b. When is it proper to talk about giving?

 c. When is it helpful to give *out loud*?

Taking action:

1) Determine when you will raise your hand and when you will be anonymous. Knowing this before the issue is raised will bring peace of mind and prevent a myriad of issues.

CHAPTER 15

IT'S A SPIRITUAL GIFT!

In His grace, God has given us different gifts for doing certain things well....If it is giving, give generously.
Romans 12:6–8

Christian bookshelves are weighed down with many writings about spiritual gifts. While we won't dissect the topic completely, let's start with a brief a summary of what spiritual gifts are before we dive into the gift of giving. There are several discussions of spiritual gifts in the New Testament: Romans 12, 1 Corinthians 12 and 14, Ephesians 4, and 1 Peter 4. Among the various lists of gifts in the Bible, the apostle Paul lists the gifts of prophecy, service, teaching, encouragement, giving, leadership, and showing mercy.

Here are some significant aspects about spiritual gifts:

- A spiritual gift is defined as a God-given capacity of every Christian to carry out the functions of the body of believers.

- The Holy Spirit gives the gifts for the benefit of the entire church body.

- While they are truly supernatural enhancements of our abilities, they are not intended for a spiritual *high*; rather, they are subtle enhancements that allow the members of the church to take care of one another in every way possible.

- We do not earn God's gifts; they are given in spite of ourselves, not because we deserve them.

- Our spiritual gifts don't provide us with any type of status within the church or a higher level of holiness or spirituality. Exercising humility is crucial to the way we serve our loving God.

- Our spiritual gifts make us sensitive to the needs around us. Acting on them is the natural result.

Imagine you are walking through the food court of a busy mall at lunchtime. Each store has a line streaming into the crowd, and people are bustling everywhere. Two young men are walking briskly toward each other carrying trays with their food and drinks. They crash into each other and fall on the floor, flipping their trays over and spilling drinks and sandwiches all over the place. A group of Christians at a nearby table witnesses the calamity unfold and each responds according to their gifting. A young man with the gift of encouragement approaches one of them and pats him on the back, telling him he is going to be okay. A girl with the gift of service quickly grabs some napkins and paper towels and kneels down to help clean up the mess. One with the gift of giving pulls a few bills out of his wallet and quietly offers to buy the unfortunate pair another meal.

Your spiritual gift is not only how you serve best but also the lens through which you see needs around you. Knowing your spiritual gift can help you understand why you are drawn to certain types of ministry and help you find your place of service. There are a great number of effective resources for discovering your gifts, such as the online tool at spiritualgifttest.com. After discerning which gifts we may have, we then need to gain experience and learn how to use them wisely.

Once you distinguish what your top two or three gifts are, you can begin the process of learning how to leverage them. Just as we have been entrusted with money and God has asked us to steward it well, we must also give an account for how we use the spiritual gifts He has given us.

THE GIFT OF GIVING

While everybody is called to give, there are those among us who have a special turbo boost in the area of generosity. Paul writes, "If [your gift] is giving, give generously" (Romans 12:8). This is not just some obscure verse in the Bible. Giving is not the redheaded stepchild among the gifts. It is also not a minor gift that God doles out to those who can't handle what some wrongly see as more *important* spiritual gifts. The God-inspired generosity is really something amazing. It is the supernaturally empowered ability to see needs other people seldom see and the skill to provide physical gifts, money, and resources in creative ways that change lives for the better.

Those blessed with the gift of giving are special people indeed. They are sensitive to the financial needs of people around them. They work behind the scenes and rarely get the attention someone with the gift of prophecy or teaching may get, nevertheless the giver is just as influential to the body of believers. While everything we've discussed in this book applies to all believers in Christ, those who have the gift of giving may resonate especially well with the lessons and stories herein. This may be you!

If God has endowed you with this gift, then you have the potential to be a blessing to people around you. There are countless men and women who have been called by God to go to some type of mission field, whether it's right in their hometown or far away. They are inspired and have the skills and experience to do the job. They are ready to go, equipped with everything except the money. Maybe you can help provide their solution financially!

TURBO CHARGING YOUR GIFTS

God works in us through our primary and secondary gifting—that is, through our top two spiritual gifts. Sally, for example, is a middle-aged accountant who is gifted in the areas of teaching and giving. She is passionate about coaching basic life skills to the homeless. Over the years, she has volunteered in her local mission shelters and made connections with dozens of women to help them get stable employment.

Sally also has the gift of giving, so she has organized her finances to allow her to be more generous. She has worked out her mission statement and built a portfolio of organizations she supports—all dedicated to helping the homeless. She gives to institutions she loves and respects that have influence locally and all over the world. Because of her gift of giving, her influence extends far beyond the reaches of her own personal platform.

If your two most prominent gifts are mercy and giving, then you will be drawn to give to ministries delivering mercy—feeding the poor, bringing clean water to villages, or starting schools. If you are gifted in administration and giving, then your portfolio will be exceptionally well organized and your giving will be directed to those who develop good leaders. If you are gifted in evangelism, then your generosity efforts will be directed toward ministers and organizations that spread the gospel of Jesus Christ.

If giving is one of your top two spiritual gifts, I have exciting news for you: the gift

> *The gift of giving turbo charges every other spiritual gift.*

of giving turbo charges every other spiritual gift. Giving boosts the influence you have through your primary gift and allows your presence to be extended far beyond what you can do on your own. By sowing the dollars God has entrusted to you, your effectiveness in the areas of your passions is multiplied!

EVERYBODY IS INCLUDED

In the many publications and websites that discuss spiritual gifts, some descriptions say the gift of giving is primarily given to the wealthy. They say that those with the gift of giving have a higher income and therefore have the ability to give. In doing so, they restrict the gift to the small percentage of people who are affluent.

This is nonsense.

Saying that the gift of giving is only for the rich is like saying the gift of evangelism is only for those who give sermons at crusades where thousands come to know Jesus. What's the first name that comes to your mind when you hear the word *evangelist*? Many people would say Billy Graham. He was arguably the greatest evangelist in history, with literally millions of people responding to the invitation to accept Jesus Christ as their personal Savior. However, there are thousands of evangelists who operate in the gift of evangelism without ever taking the stage.

My friend Markco Miller worked for Heartland Financial USA, but he considered his *real* job to be evangelism. Markco lived to tell people about Jesus. Every breath he took enabled him to tell people about Jesus. Throughout his life, Markco made every attempt to bring the gospel of Jesus Christ to everyone he knew. He was a dynamic character and made a splash wherever he went. When we were at a restaurant together, he would make sure the waitress heard about Jesus. When we planned a simple event for church, he would invite a dozen people and made sure the gospel was front and center in the meeting. Markco did everything he possibly could have done to share the message of the gospel of Jesus for all his days. He did not have national acclaim, but he exercised his gift to the best of his ability with exuberance and energy.

If you were to make a list of all the people who came to Jesus through Markco's efforts, it would be quite a long list. If you were to hold that list up to Billy Graham's, however, Markco's efforts would look embarrassingly small. Does that diminish the work Markco did? Absolutely not! Does it mean only the big evangelists are really evangelizing? Not by any means!

Likewise, why would we think that only those who are giving in high dollar amounts would be the ones who are effective in the spiritual gift of giving? It does seem that those who give in large amounts have bigger and better stories, but this is not how God views money. God looks at the heart, not the number of zeroes written on a check.

Givers have the opportunity to be a significant blessing. Does that mean every person with the gift of giving has put their financial affairs in order and lives below their means so they can exercise their gift? Absolutely not! My friend Carl has struggled with finances his whole life. He works three jobs to pay his bills and gets by week to week. His credit score is nothing to brag about, and he struggles to take care of his wife and kids. They are deeply in debt, using one credit card to pay off another, and seem to be in no position to help others. Yet, when his mother's minivan died, he didn't hesitate to give her his own car—to his own detriment. His passion to give outweighed his financial discipline.

I should add one warning to this, though: if you're married, don't make huge giving commitments without talking it over with your spouse. Some people say giving spontaneously is the best way to build your faith. When you give away your rent money without knowing how your bills will be taken care of, you are putting your faith in God to provide, right? God does provide, and He has challenged us to test Him in this. Without great communication, however, the result of this type of giving is often chaos in the marital relationship. When the husband is frugal and the wife gives or spends more than they are able (or vice versa), marital strife is just around the corner. Financial security is important in a marriage. When a husband or wife spends or gives without the security that the bills will be covered, their relationship suffers. That's why, for the sake of the health of a marriage, giving should be done together as a part of a plan. When we follow God's plan for our giving through wise planning and strategy, we can have marital harmony.

The proper exercise of any spiritual gift requires discipline. Teachers, for example, must spend many hours and organize their lives around preparation time to teach effectively. The same principles apply to giving. When a family (regardless of their income level) follows a budget, is out of debt, and has financial peace, they don't worry about how to pay for their next meal. They can comfortably give out of their surplus. This is a much healthier way to give.

The giving that the couple engages in is then done as a team effort, together with wisdom. This type of giving is no less spiritual than giving without a plan, and it provides for a healthy relationship between a husband and wife.

NO JUDGING

Each of us gives differently, whether it's to an abbey in Alabama or a zoo in Zaire. We should avoid comparison and embrace the differences in our giving.

A group of eight women sit in a circle in their weekly small-group Bible study. Bobbi, the leader, encourages each of them to share what they are passionate about and walks the group through a discussion about giving. Eloise takes the plunge first and shares that she just provided $50 toward a camp scholarship for her high-school youth group. Jackie is excited about a hospital in Zimbabwe and has made a donation of thousands of dollars. Bobbi knows them both well and points out that they are following direction from God and operating in their spiritual gift of giving. More people share as they go around the circle; some indicate that they don't give outside their local church. It becomes evident that some have minimal interest in giving, while others have centered their lives around it. Inevitably, an undertone of comparison creeps in.

Bobbi spends the rest of their time together teaching that, since God views money differently than we do, we should embrace our differences, view money the way God does, and worship Him in the process. She points out that there is no place for ranking one person's giving over another's. At the end of the discussion, the group is amazed with how much there is to learn about giving in general as well as the wealth of opportunities for exercising generosity. They commit to working together to learn more about the giving process. It is possible to be open about our passions and our giving without judgment or resentment staining the process.

When we realize that each of us views things through the lens of our spiritual gifts and extend grace to our friends, we discover we can learn from them. What one person may see as an opportunity to give, another views as an opportunity to extend mercy or teach. Often, all the above are needed. Working as a team, the body of Christ can build one another up.

LEVERAGE YOUR GIFT

You may have the gift of giving. If this is your calling, it is your responsibility to leverage it. Take some time to develop your stewardship philosophy. With Jesus walking next to you, prioritize your finances and look through your budget. Build your giving portfolio and be ready to work through the pitfalls inherent to the process. Just like the gifted musician practices and makes plenty of mistakes along the way, so every giver will have their share of blunders. We improve our effectiveness through experience. Dive in and grow your influence in this gift with practice and diligence.

Looking inside:

1) Have you ever thought that your focus on giving was a little crazy?

   a. When God asks people to do things, there is often no way to do them in our own power, and obedience is seen as crazy or radical.

   b. Be ready to practice lifestyle generosity!

2) When have you seen the spiritual gift of giving act to turbo charge the other gifts?

Taking action:

1) Take a spiritual gift assessment and list your top three gifts. If giving is on the list, were you surprised?

CHAPTER 16

PUTTING IT ALL TOGETHER

He asked Jesus, "And who is my neighbor?"

Luke 10:29

Giving involves much more than wrapping a present and delivering it to a friend. It is also more complex than simply going online and making a donation. As we've seen, establishing a relationship between the donor and recipient takes wisdom and effort. While there are plenty of ways we can take our eyes off the ball and exercise poor giving, it can also be a beautiful expression of God's love when it is done well.

ROOFING FOR JESUS

After a long day of showing houses and dealing with clients in Dubuque, Iowa, Karen Hudek was finally on her way home. As a real estate agent, she knew the homes in her city like the back of her hand. She enjoyed seeing the springtime flowers resting in planters and people enjoying the sunny evening as they strolled down the street. Nearby, a blue tarpaulin partially covered the wrinkled shingles on a roof of a white house. As she drove home, her mind wandered off to recipe options for dinner that evening.

The following morning, Karen began her morning ritual with time in the Bible and praying through a list of needs for her family and friends. As she picked up her keys to head to work, she was stopped in her tracks. She felt God saying, "Karen, you need to go put a roof on that person's house."

As she heard the words, a visual image of the white house covered with a blue tarp came to life. She had no question that this was God speaking directly to her. She had heard His voice many times before and knew how to distinguish her own silly ideas from God's divine direction. There was also no question about which house God was talking about. For Karen, this was a clear message; however, she didn't quite understand. She hadn't been asking God if she should help that person. She hadn't even thought about the tarp on the roof, but God had clearly given her instructions to put a roof on that person's house.

Karen paused and prayed, *Okay, God.*

Her plan for the day had taken a turn. Sitting behind the wheel of her minivan, she thought about what it takes to put on a new roof. How would she get it done? How much would it cost? Who should she call first? She thought through a list of contacts that could help and dialed Bill Brown, a contractor friend.

"Hello," came the masculine voice on the other end of the line.

"Good morning, it's Karen," she said.

"It's good to hear from you. How can I help?"

"How much would it cost to put a new roof on a house on Rhomberg Street?"

Bill replied, "I don't know. There are lots of different houses down there, but tell me the address."

Karen's face turned pale, "I don't know the address."

"What? What do you mean?" Bill said.

She told him, "I was just driving by and noticed a tarp on the roof, and they must have water coming into the house. So, I'm feeling like God is telling me to buy them a new roof."

Bill hesitated, having never heard a story like this. "Okay. Who lives there?"

"I don't know." She said.

There was a long pause.

"Let me get this straight: you want to spend a bunch of money on a new roof for some people you don't know?"

Karen sunk down in her seat a little. "Yep, that's about it."

Bill said, "Well, it doesn't hurt to look; let's meet downtown." Later that morning, she climbed into Bill's truck and they drove to the house. Bill saw the tarp, assessed the situation, and said, "I've been doing this for a long time. My sidewalk estimate is $5,500."

Karen was sad. She replied, "I only have $3,000."

Bill said, "Don't worry about that. If God is telling you to do this, He'll make a way. Let's go talk with them."

Karen had a streak of boldness as they knocked on the door. A woman opened the door and they made their introductions and explained that she would like to fix their roof. She responded, "I'm sorry, but we don't have any money."

"You don't understand," she replied. "This is something I want to do for you."

"What?"

Karen said, "I want to hire Bill, a contractor, to fix your roof for you." She told them about what God had impressed on her that morning and that she was just there to help.

Tears roll down her cheeks. "No way! People don't do that. I'm disabled and can't work."

She invited Karen and Bill inside Bill looked around the living room with a contractor's eye. She went on to say, "Just today we are traveling to Iowa City to go the doctor. If you want to bless us that way, we would love it."

After making a promise she didn't know how to fulfill, Karen and Bill headed back to the truck. Bill withdrew $300 from his wallet, wrapped it around his business card, and gave it to Karen. He looked her in the eye and said, "Go back inside and tell them that this is to help with their trip to Iowa City."

With wind in their sails, they made plans to start the following day. Bill filled out the paperwork for a building permit at City Hall. He told the clerk the story. "A lady is donating a roof for this family. She doesn't know them at all, but God told her to put a roof on the house."

They talked for a few minutes about the situation, and the clerk broke into tears. She filled out the paperwork and said, "Here you go. And we're giving you this building permit free of charge!"

The work began. As they tore off the roof, word spread around the neighborhood about a construction project someone was donating. People came to see what was going on, and the new roof became the talk of the town. Some of the homeowners' nephews who lived nearby volunteered to help. They trimmed hedges and worked on the lawn.

Bill drove his truck full of old, worn shingles to the landfill and shared the story with the cashier. He responded, "Go dump your stuff, no charge."

As Bill's crew nailed on new shingles, he noticed that the front door needed to be replaced and the lattice was falling apart. He visited the contractor's counter at the local hardware store and spoke with the manager. "God told this lady to put a new roof on this house, and . . ." He told the whole story then asked, "Can you help us out?"

The manager responded, "Go ahead and get a new door, new lattice, plus anything else you need for the house. No charge."

The next day, Bill called up a burly contractor buddy named Wolffe who specialized in gutter work and told him the story. He concluded, "Hey, Wolffe, you owe me one. Come over here and put gutters and downspouts on this house for free."

Wolffe graciously responded, "I'll be right there."

The whole project took a little more than a week. Karen spent her $3,000, but the investment was far greater than that.

A few weeks later, as Karen was headed home after work, a rainstorm began to drench the city. She drove down Rhomberg Street and saw the beautiful white house, and her heart filled with joy. She pulled over, walked up to the front door, and knocked. The homeowner came to the door, saw Karen, and burst into tears.

After a few moments, he said, "Karen, I used to have nightmares when it rained. The water would come in, and there was nothing that I could do to stop it. Now I'm the happiest guy alive. I can come out here on my porch and listen to the rain, knowing that it's not coming into my house."

His wife joined the conversation. "We want to know about this God who told you to do this for us. We've never known God to be generous, kind, and loving. We've never known God like that."

They talked for an hour. Karen told them about Jesus and His love for us. They asked, "Would you take us to church with you?" The following Sunday, Karen picked them up in her minivan. After church, they asked, "We want to know this God. Who would drive over here and do something like this at their own cost?"

The couple dedicated their lives to Jesus Christ. Eventually, their entire extended family became followers of Christ, as well. Karen developed a new routine of picking up their family on the way to church every week. Their relationship grew as they joined together in friendship.

GIVING WELL

Karen started by responding to a simple statement, "Put a roof on that house." This God-inspired directive turned into a large project that grew to involve a whole neighborhood. The result was not only a house with a new roof; an entire extended family was changed for eternity.

Karen wasn't running an organization called Roofs for Downtown. She didn't have carpenters on staff or use a smooth application process to evaluate people's financial need and review who needs a roof and where she should focus her efforts. She didn't form such an organization after this experience, either. Karen simply acted in obedience to a call from her loving God. She already had her finances in order and had a certain amount she could give spontaneously. She knew her personal stewardship philosophy and understood the types of projects she would support and what she wouldn't.

When God said, "Put a roof on that house," she didn't shy away from the fact that this was God's instruction, nor did she hesitate or delay. She went right to work.

We often focus on sacrifice when we talk about giving. When we give, we choose to hand money over to someone else rather than using it ourselves. This is a sacrifice. God has a lot to teach about sacrifice, but the Bible also says it is better to *obey* than to sacrifice. First Samuel 15:22 says, "What is more pleasing to the LORD: your burnt offerings and sacrifices or your obedience to his voice? Listen! Obedience is better than sacrifice, and submission is better than offering the fat of rams." Sacrifice is definitely an important spiritual act, but obedience is the key.

> *It is better to obey than to sacrifice.*

Karen knew the voice of her loving God. When she heard God speak, she obeyed.

Looking inside:

1) Imagine Jesus standing beside Karen throughout this story. What would He say at each step along the way?

2) Read James 2:12–18. If faith is shown by deeds, how is your faith seen in what you do?

Taking action:

1) Read Luke 10:25–37 (the Parable of the Good Samaritan).

    a. What was Jesus talking about when He said we should love our neighbor as ourselves?

    b. Who is your neighbor?

    c. How do you show them love?

    d. Do you think it made sense for the Samaritan to care for the man on the road?

2) Have you ever heard God tell you to do something that doesn't seem to make sense? What did you do with God's unusual request?

CHAPTER 17

TRUE LIFE

Tell them to use their money to do good. They should be rich in good works and generous to those in need, always being ready to share with others.

1 Timothy 6:18

"Fight the good fight for the true faith," Paul said to his accomplished young apprentice, Timothy (1 Timothy 6:12). What follows this statement is one of the greatest explanations of generosity ever written. Taken as a whole, this passage explains what our attitude toward money should be.

Although the "fight the good fight" statement has been taken out of context and misused, the good fight of faith is an all-encompassing battle cry for the young man's life. Paul said it well:

Fight the good fight for the true faith. Hold tightly to the eternal life to which God has called you, which you have declared so well before many witnesses. …Teach those who are rich in this world not to be proud and not to trust in their money, which is so unreliable. Their trust should be in God, who richly gives us all we need for our enjoyment. Tell them to use their money to do good. They should be rich in good works and generous to those in need, always being ready to share with others. By doing this they will be storing up their treasure as a good foundation for the future so that they may experience true life. (1 Timothy 6:12, 17–19)

There is a lot going on in this short passage. Bear with me as we break it down bit-by-bit and get to what Paul was trying to convey to his protégé.

First, Paul revealed God's character. Remember, Paul had a life-changing experience on the road to Damascus where overwhelming light blinded him and Jesus Himself confronted him. Paul's worship is reminiscent of that awesome experience with God.

At this point in his letter, I envision Paul as if he were traveling at ninety miles an hour, all wound up, with his hair blown back. He was fully charged in worship of the almighty God, who loves us dearly. It is at this point in his worship of God that Paul talked about the wealthy. He said to teach those who are rich not to trust in their money or be proud of it. Their trust should be in God.

When Paul said this, he was not changing the subject. This is not a separate part of the letter that we can cut apart and separate from the worship of God. Paul continued with his literary flow and said that those who have wealth should worship God instead of their money. Indeed, they should worship God *with* their wealth! This is 100 percent consistent with what he had been saying in the previous lines. Jesus is our hope, our life, and our reason for being. We receive each breath from Him. How can we possibly look at our own accumulation of possessions and congratulate ourselves? It doesn't compute. Therefore, we should look at any wealth or possessions we have in light of the love of the awesome God who owns everything.

Paul instructed Timothy to tell those with wealth to use their money for other people, to be rich in good works, and to be generous to those in need. This play on words is almost trite in its simplicity. Nonetheless, it placed the importance of abundance not on the accumulation of wealth but on doing things that please God with the resources He has provided. Money cannot purchase joy. While every salesperson promulgates the myth that they sell happiness, joy comes through using what God has provided to be generous to others in need.

Notice that Paul did not condemn the rich. He did not blame them for having resources. He did not declare the gospel according to Robin Hood, where the rich are evil and distributing to the poor is the essence of salvation. Rather, Paul continued in his discussion of the wealthy and echoed Jesus' message in Matthew 6: "By doing this they will be storing up their treasure as a good foundation for the future so that they may experience true life" (1 Timothy 6:19). What just happened? Did you see that? Paul pulled the ultimate quote that we have been using throughout our discussion of stewardship as we talked about the heavenly bank account, but Paul took it to the next level!

Jesus said we should not lay up treasure for ourselves where moth and rust destroy; rather, we should lay up treasure for ourselves in heaven. This heavenly bank account, a reward for giving, is based on faith in our loving God. Paul affirmed Jesus' concept that giving here on earth is storing up treasure in a heavenly bank account. When we make a deposit here, God records it for us there.

Please understand that the amount of every deposit is measured in obedience (not dollars), and we cannot make a withdrawal on this side of heaven. It can make a big splash when a rich person gives a small percentage of his income; however, God looks at the *heart*—not the *splash*. When the widow gave tiny copper coins, she gave all she had to live on. By her act of generosity, Jesus proclaimed that she had given more than the rich who were dropping in heavy loads of gold.

Paul's teaching grew to the final point, "So that they may experience true life" (1 Timothy 6:19). When our lives are focused on our sovereign God and we are generous with the resources He has provided, we give in faith and store up treasure in heaven. This process is taking hold of that "true life." That which is truly life is all wrapped up in taking the security we have in money and being generous with it through faith in our wonderful God.

Wow!

There aren't many times that we are taught about the meaning of life. If the apostle Paul says we are experiencing "true life," I have to assume that worshiping God is why we are here on this planet. And a big part of how we do worship Him is through generosity.

BEING CHRIST IN THE WORLD

Stewarding money is not easy. It takes discipline and work. It's an incredible responsibility and not one to take lightly. When God has given us gifts, whether they are talents, spiritual insight, or even something physical that we can hold and touch, it is inherent in the fabric of our relationship with Him that we use those gifts as if they are representatives of God Himself.

This applies to all aspects of our lives, not just money. It applies to our relationships with our spouses and children. We need to take seriously the Scripture's challenge for husbands to love their wives as Christ loved the church. I continually need to prioritize my relationship with Anna so she knows where she stands in my life. As an outpouring of love from the Father Himself, I will love her with everything I have. She knows this and does not doubt my dedication to her, and she knows how I will respond to most any situation. She is my priority, and she knows it.

It also applies in our vocations. When we spend forty hours a week or more in some type of job, we pour our hearts into our work. This is not necessarily because of a true love for the work, but rather the results that the work brings: a steady wage, status, and hopefully, the satisfaction of a job done well. When we work in our secular vocations as extensions of an overwhelming love of Christ and work in our jobs because we are actually working for the awesome God, our Father, then our work is an act of worship to Him.

The application extends to our volunteer activities in community or church. Rather than volunteering out of a sense of obligation or duty (or because nobody else will do the work), we give our time to serve God and others because our lives represent the amazing Jesus who lives in us. The light of Jesus shines through us as we serve.

Finally, it applies to the way we steward our finances. In the preceding pages, I've allowed you to peek through a keyhole into my family's life and other people's stories. Anna and I are in the process of living with a heart of obedience to a loving God. For me, it started way before the challenge God gave me on Goose Island; it began in a parking lot in the backseat of a Buick when I prayed with my mother to submit my life to Jesus Christ. The rest has been birthed from a life of saying, "Yes, Lord!"

God has called us to a life of giving, a life of sharing what we have, whether small or large amounts, with those around us. Imagine living with Jesus standing right next to you, complete with His beard, white robe, and blue sash, encouraging you every step along the way. When we are tempted to hold back some of the proceeds for ourselves, He will simply nudge us to be honest. When we are burned, He will teach as He leads and guides us. When we are unmotivated, He will bring people who have specific needs we can help with into our lives.

Every penny that passes through our hands tells a story about our relationship with God. Generosity allows us to give Him our hearts and take hold of *true life*. Whatever God lays upon your heart in the realm of finances, follow through with it. The rewards of honest generosity are worth the sacrifice.

Test Him! Give abundantly and see what God does!

Looking inside:

1) Where are you in your journey of generosity?

    a. Are you in the process of drawing near to God and giving routinely?

    b. Are you discovering the eternal blessings of laying up treasure in heaven?

2) How is giving an act of worship?

    a. In what way does our generosity reflect the heart of God?

    b. Do we have to have everything together in order to live lives of generosity?

3) If not, what is holding you back?

Taking action:

1) Name two practical ways you can test God in giving. If you can't think of any, review the questions in the previous chapters and commit to one action point.

2) Implement it today.

ACKNOWLEDGMENTS

Scripture says our plans will fail for lack of counsel but succeed with many advisors (Proverbs 15:22). I have not walked on this journey alone. I am indebted to a number of friends and family members for helping me through this process of understanding how God wants us to handle His resources. Without the input of the following trusted advisors, the book in your hands would be woefully inadequate.

Rich VanderSande gave early instruction about the concept of the *finish line* and has continued providing guidance for me in all things financial. Mary Pudaite Keating played a major role with her knowledge of writing and her unique ability to connect to many people in the world of generosity. She helped me transform this book from a manuscript that sits on my computer to a book that reaches out to the masses.

I can't thank my family enough. By bringing along an early draft of this book, I unwittingly turned a weeklong family reunion into a mini-financial conference. My brothers, Dennis and John, along with their wives, Jennifer and Kim, pacified my external processing with deep discussions about every nook and cranny of generosity. They revealed tremendous pearls of wisdom from their own lives and provided stories of generosity I hadn't previously known. My loving parents, Denny and Twink, were indispensable in this process. With their decades of living generously, they were happy to watch their kids wade through the waters and lent their wisdom. Their many years of writing and editing experience helped bring the discussions into readable prose.

A number of dear friends gave wisdom and insight as they endured various draft versions of the manuscript: Dr. Shanu Kothari, Dr. Jon Zlabek, Neil Ihde, Kurt and Patti Behning, Dan and Sarah Allison, Brian and Lynette Schatz, Brian Pendleton, Tami Jansen, Mark Derber, Karen Hudek, Tim Williams, Dennis Rima, Boyd and Fran Baker, and Robert Kimble. I truly appreciate the artistic work of Ryan Winkelman and Jim Minor with the graphics and cover design.

I know I left out many who have been with me over the years. Please know that I appreciate all the education and correction I have received along the way.

But the one solitary person who has been and continues to be my biggest help in everything I do is my lovely wife, Anna. She inspired me to get started, helped me process complex ideas, edited, connected me with others, and encouraged me at every step along the way.

APPENDIX 1

FURTHER READING

I highly recommend the following books about biblical stewardship:

Alcorn, Randy. *The Law of Rewards Giving What You Can't Keep to Gain What You Can't Lose.* Carol Stream, IL: Tyndale House Publishers. 1989.

Alcorn, Randy. *The Treasure Principle: Discovering the Secret of Joyful Giving.* Sisters, OR: Multnomah Publishers. 2001

Anderson, Jeff. *Plastic Donuts: A Fresh Perspective on Gifts.* Acceptable Gift, Inc., 2012.

Blue, Ron, and Michael Blue. *Master Your Money: A Step-By-Step Plan for Experiencing Financial Contentment.* Chicago: Moody Publishers. 2016.

Corbett, Steve, and Brian Fikkert. *When Helping Hurts: How to Alleviate Poverty without Hurting the Poor—and Yourself.* Chicago: Moody Publishers. 2009.

Cortines, John, and Gregory Baumer. *God and Money: How We Discovered True Riches at Harvard Business School.* Carson, CA: Rose Publishing. 2016.

DeWitt, Andrew. *Give Your Best: How Willem Charles Transformed His Haitian Village from Poverty in Voodoo to Prosperity in Christianity.* CreateSpace. 2010.

Harper, Todd. *Abundant: Experiencing the Incredible Journey of Generosity.* United States of America. 2016.

Ingram, Chip. *The Genius of Generosity: Lessons from a Secret Pact Between Two Friends.* Generous Church. 2011.

Lewis, C. S. *Mere Christianity.* Copper Kettle. 1943.

Link, E. G. "Jay." *To Whom Much Is Given: Navigating the Ten Life Dilemmas Affluent Christians Face.* Xulon Press. 2009.

Nowery, Kirk. *The Giving Christian: Sowing Seeds for an Eternal Harvest.* Camarillo, CA: Spire Resources Inc. 2005.

Nowery, Kirk. *The Stewardship of Life: Making the Most of All That You Have and All That You Are.* Camarillo, CA: Spire Resources Inc. 2004.

Nouwen, Henri. *A Spirituality of Fundraising.* Nashville: Upper Room Books. 2010.

Platt, David. *Radical: Taking Back Your Faith from the American Dream.* Colorado Springs, CO: WaterBrook Multnomah, Inc. 2010.

Stanley, Andy. *Fields of Gold: A Place Beyond Your Deepest Fears, A Prize Beyond Your Wildest Imagination.* Wheaton, IL: Tyndale House Publishers, Inc. 2004.

Sutherland, Dave, and Kirk Nowery. *The 33 Laws of Stewardship: Principles for a Life of True Fulfillment.* Camarillo, CA: Spire Resources Inc. 2003.

VanderSande, Rich, and Mark Matson. *The Dirty, Filthy Lies My Broker Taught Me and 101 Truths About Money & Investing.* Cincinnati: McGriff Publishing. 2005.

Willmer, Wesley K. *Revolution in Generosity: Transforming Stewards to Be Rich Toward God.* Chicago: Moody Publishers. 2008.

RESOURCES

National Christian
FOUNDATION®

Our team at the National Christian Foundation (NCF) helps generous givers like you simplify their giving, multiply their impact, and experience the joy of sending more to their favorite causes than they ever dreamed possible. Together, since 1982, we have mobilized more than $10 billion in grants for 55,000 charities who are doing amazing work around the corner and around the world.

NCFGiving.com

GENEROUS GIVING
Finding a Joy Unexpected.

Founded in 2000 by The Maclellan Foundation, Generous Giving's mission is to spread the biblical message of generosity in order to grow generous givers. They endeavor to provide safe, solicitation-free environments for conversations with peers around generosity and for powerfully connecting givers to God's heart. They never seek donations, permit solicitation at events, or award grants. You can find a variety of encouraging video stories on generosity available for free on their website.

Generousgiving.org

Stewardship Legacy Coaching LLC

Many financially-blessed people want their legacy to be a blessing to their children and grandchildren, but they are unsure how to navigate the complexities of transferring not only their wealth, but their wisdom, family values and virtues. They want their wealth to be a blessing, not a curse; to help, not harm, their children & grandchildren. People get all fired up about how they can change the world, but without practical help on how navigate the complexity of financial, relational & sometimes highly emotional issues, results will not be optimized. Stewardship Legacy Coaching has a trained team of Legacy Coaches with a Christ-centered worldview who speak the language of generosity. They can help you connect the dots between your legacy dreams and aspirations and your personal financial picture with information, inspiration, and implementation to help ensure your legacy inspires a thriving family, for generations to come.

Stewardshiplegacy.com.

NOTES

Chapter 1

1 Scripture references to the tithe: Genesis 28:22; Numbers 18:21, 24, 26, 28, 32; Deuteronomy 12:6, 11, 17; 14:22, 23, 24, 25, 28; 26:1, 12; 2 Chronicles 31:5, 6, 12; Nehemiah 10:37, 38; 12:44; 13:5, 12; Amos 4:4; Malachi 3:8; Matthew 23:23; Luke 11:42; Hebrews 7:5, 8, 9, and 7:1.

2 C. S. Lewis, *Mere Christianity* (Copper Kettle, 1943), 49.

3 Scriptures that refer to the treatment of widows: Exodus 22:22, 24; Deuteronomy 10:18; 14:29; 16:11, 14; 24:17, 19, 20, 21; 26:12, 13; 27:19.

Chapter 4

1 Randy Alcorn, *The Treasure Principle: Discovering the Secret of Joyful Giving* (Sisters, OR: Multnomah Publishers, 2001), 73.

2 Andy Stanley, *Fields of Gold: A Place Beyond Your Deepest Fears, a Prize Beyond Your Wildest Imagination* (Wheaton, IL: Tyndale House Publishers, Inc., 2004), 22–27.

3 John Cortines and Gregory Baumer, *God and Money: How We Discovered True Riches at Harvard Business School* (Carson, CA: Rose Publishing, 2016), 240–49.

4   Michael Richardson, *Amazing Faith: The Authorized Biography of Bill Bright, Founder of Campus Crusade for Christ* (Colorado Springs, CO: WaterBrook Press, 2001), 59–60.

5   *Generous Giving*, "Sheela's Story—2018 Spring Celebration of Generosity," accessed July 30, 2018, https://generousgiving.org/media/videos/sheelas-story.

6   Nathan Bomey, "Domino's founder Tom Monaghan pledges half of his fortune to charity," *The Ann Arbor News*, August 5, 2010, http://www.annarbor.com/business-review/billionaire-tom-monaghan-pledges-half-of-his-fortune-to-charity/.

7   Stanley, *Fields of Gold*, 112–15.

8   Stanley, *Fields of Gold*, 123–27.

9   *Generous Giving*, "Thomas Maclellan—Creating a Lasting Legacy," accessed July 30, 2018, https://generousgiving.org/media/videos/thomas-maclellan-creating-a-lasting-legacy.

10 Ron Blue and Michael Blue, *Master Your Money: A Step-By-Step Plan for Experiencing Financial Contentment* (Chicago: Moody Publishers, 2016), 21–22.

11 Ron Blue, "How Much Is Enough?" *Wisdom for Wealth. For Life*, Fall 2017, http://www.ronblue.com/Portals/0/Wisdom-for-Wealth-For-Life-Newsletter-Fall-2017.pdf.

Chapter 6

1   Steve Corbett and Brian Fikkert, *When Helping Hurts: How to Alleviate Poverty without Hurting the Poor—and Yourself* (Chicago: Moody Publishers, 2009), 28.

Chapter 8

1 Scripture references where the name Jehovah-Jireh is used: Psalm 37:4, 25; Matthew 6:25–34; Romans 8:37; Ephesians 1:3; and Philippians 4:19.

Chapter 9

1 John Breech, "Derek Carr reveals the first thing he's going to splurge on with his new contract," *CBSSports.com*, June 23, 2017, https://www.cbssports.com/nfl/news/derek-carr-reveals-the-first-thing-hes-going-to-splurge-on-with-his-new-contract/.

Chapter 10

1 Joseph P. Lash, *The Story of Helen Keller and Anne Sullivan Macy* (New York: Delacorte Press/Seymour Lawrence, 1980), 489.

Chapter 11

1 Loren Cunningham and Janice Rogers, *Is That Really You, God? Hearing the Voice of God* (Seattle: YWAM Publishing, 1984), 132.

2 Cunningham and Rogers, *Is That Really You, God?*, 147.

Chapter 14

1 Anna Johansson, "The Numbers Are In: Corporate Generosity Boosts Employee Engagement," May 2, 2017, https://www.triplepundit.com/2017/05/numbers-corporate-generosity-boosts-employee-engagement/.

2 Dictionary.com, "Philanthropy," accessed July 25, 2018, http://www.dictionary.com/browse/philanthropy.